Ben's Limehouse

BEN THOMAS

RAGGED SCHOOL MUSEUM TRUST
1998

First published 1987
Second edition 1998
Ragged School Museum Trust
46-50 Copperfield Road
London E3 4RR

Acknowledgements

As the photographs, illustrations, text and captions in this
second edition are unaltered from the first edition the
Ragged School Museum Trust would like to thank all
those individuals and organisations who have allowed us
to re-use their material.
We also thank West Ferry Printers for their contribution to
the cost of this second edition.

Printed by Adept Press Ltd. Tel: 0181-998 2247
A commercial litho printing company staffed by deaf people and run as a co-operative

LIST OF ILLUSTRATIONS

CONTENTS

EARLY MEMORIES

An upstairs front room, a yellow and red flag on a plain wooden pole being put out of a window. The feel of that rough bunting rubbing against me at times I imagine I feel now. I have found out since that it was a yellow flag with a red lion on it. That is the earliest thought that I remember. Also the hustle and bustle of people, and excitement of them, as they were putting it out of the window.

Was it the relief of Mafeking being celebrated? The Crimean War ended? Or the Coronation of King George V and Queen Mary? If it was the Coronation of King George and Queen Mary, I was only three years old, for I was born on the 1st of June 1907, but it must have been earlier than the Coronation, for I remember the Catholic Infants School that I went to. Yes, that was my earliest memory, playing with sand in a tin tray, playing with a ball on a piece of elastic. The ball was silver paper, filled with sawdust, and held together with coloured cotton netting, each child having a different coloured ball, to learn colours. I remember making letters and figures in the tray of sand, to help us learn letters and numbers. We also had wooden beads on a wire, which were also coloured. Then my next class, where we had slates, and a slate pencil to write or draw with. One side of the slate, which was in a wooden frame, had rows of three lines on it, on which we were taught to write our small and capital letters, and learn to spell. The scratching of them slate pencils on the slate, I can hear and feel now.

There were a lot of pictures of animals on the wall in one class, I think it was the babies' class. For I remember the rocking horse distinctly, with its wicker cane seats, which we were rocked in sometimes in the afternoon, but in the morning our name was written on our lunches which we brought to school, and put in the rocking horse seats.

My first teacher's name was Miss Cassey. Then Miss Lyons, and Miss Goggins was the head mistress. Miss Cassey was short compared to Miss Lyons and Miss Goggins, and was much gayer. Miss Lyons was pleasant compared to Miss Goggins, who was as tall as Miss Lyons, but had thin drawn cheeks, and must have had delicate health, as she was so thin. The other thing I remember well was Miss Goggins' bustle and face veil, when going and coming to school. The veil was in a mauve colour.

3

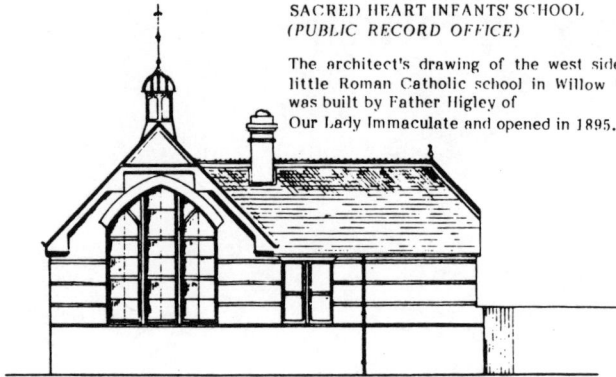

SACRED HEART INFANTS' SCHOOL
(PUBLIC RECORD OFFICE)

The architect's drawing of the west side of the little Roman Catholic school in Willow Row which was built by Father Higley of Our Lady Immaculate and opened in 1895.

The school, which was in Willow Row, had no upper floors, and was of three classes or rooms, the top class being the biggest. You went into the school by an alley, on one side there were two room cottages with front gardens, some had big trees in them. The school caretaker and cleaner lived in the first one, and they had a large variety of flowers in their garden.

Around the school were other little cottages, and that was called the Orchard, as at one time it had all been farm land. Even the street that I lived in at the time was called Nightingale Lane, but after called Brightlingsea Place.

When I was about four, I went to Poplar Hospital with rheumatic fever. I remember crying a lot in there, and the song that I learned there was, 'He Opened His Mouth Too Wide'.

The toys I remember having was a wooden Noah's ark, with wooden painted animals, a box of bricks, lead soldiers, cardboard stage with coloured figures, wooden top and peg top, paints, crayons, scrap book, skittles, a clockwork train with rails to run on, a wooden arch with marbles, and a wooden hoop. Most girls and boys had their own hoop with them all the time, and bigger boys had iron hoops. Wooden hoops, from two feet wide, which increased in size 'till they were taller than five feet tall. I had a tin lantern, and the boy who lived down stairs had a magic lantern, illuminated by a candle, he charged $\frac{1}{4}$d a show, and it fascinated me. I had plenty of books, and being able to read so young, I had a lot of story books, our house had fiction and non fiction, as both my parents were well educated, though they paid 1d a week to go to school. My eldest brother won a scholarship. I had three brothers and three sisters, I was the youngest, and loved reading fiction and non-fiction, especially about engineering, chemistry and science.

4

THE RIVER AND CANALS

How distinctly I remember the balloons coming over the river from Crystal Palace, mostly when I was sitting on the steps of Duke Shore, where I also used to look at the different craft as they passed up and down the river. How busy the river was then! Big sailing ships and big steam boats, with one, two or even three funnels, and guided up and down by a tug, or if very big, two tugs. The lightermen rowing the barges up and down the river, worked very hard. Also going by were the sailing barges, which used to look a fine sight in full sail. And how the men worked hard, as they tacked the boats in the wind, and went from one side of the Thames to the other. Some of the sailing barges had the skipper's family on board, I have seen as many as six children, besides parents, a dog, cat and sometimes a bird. My father was a skipper of a sailing barge at one time, and he used to go over to Holland, Belgium and France sometimes. He was a seven year apprenticed lighterman. He also had the freedom of the River Thames. He left the river to be a tattooist, though our house was always full of ropes, tackles and all sorts of marine gear.

LIMEHOUSE FROM THE RIVER THAMES
(ROYAL COMMISSION ON THE HISTORICAL MONUMENTS OF ENGLAND)

Taken about 1910, the photograph shows the 'stumpy' rigged sailing barge CLYDE, owned by Grays chalk quarries, going up river with Sparks the barge builders to the left and Brightlingsea Buildings behind and, to the right, St. Anne's Church tower behind Taylor Walker's Barley Mow Brewery.

The Limehouse Cut and the Regent's Canal were busy with sailing and canal barges, which were laden with timber, coal, refuse, machinery and lot of other things I can't remember. The narrow canal barges' holds were covered in by a steep tarpaulin roof, so I never saw what they carried. If pride was taken in the canal barges, they used to look quite bright and gay, with the bright coloured flowers and designs that were painted on them. Even the buckets and tiller poles had floral designs on them. Some ropes that were rarely used were as white as snow, and neatly coiled on top of the hatch roof. When you were on a canal bridge, and you looked over, you could see down the hatches of the canal barges, or monkey barges as we used to call them, and how bright and clean some of them were! The brass shining bright besides glass ornaments, fire stoves well blackened, and hand painted floral designs on their mirrors. Long and narrow they were, and how they brought up a family on them, I don't know, but I have seen as many as four children on them.

I used to play a lot on the Thames shore, paddling, swimming, climbing on the barges, catching fish or tiddlers as we called them collecting firewood for our mother's copper, to boil clothes in, searching for old coins or things of interest to us boys. Throwing a tin can in the water, then trying to hit it until it sunk. If there were a lot of boys, we made up sides for that. Shouting and waving to the pleasure boats, such as the Royal Sovereign, the Ich Dien, the Golden Eagle and the Golden Sovereign. These pleasure boats were big paddles steamers, and went to Southend, Margate, Ramsgate, the Isle of Wight, Calais, Boulogne and other places. They mostly started from the Tower, and only in Summer. It used to be a wonderful sight to see the boats all lit up at night coming home. Sometimes we used to hear the band playing on them

Girls as well as boys used to play on the shore sometimes, mostly paddling, sitting on the stones if it was very warm, collecting firewood and waving to the pleasure boats. Like the boys, some were barefooted. When the tide was low, we were able to walk from Kidney Stairs to the Dyke as we called it when we were young, but I've found out since that it's the Limekiln Dock. Of course we went to Duke Stairs more than Kidney Stairs, as we could watch the men who worked for Sparks the barge builders, building and repairing the barges. When a barge was built, the ribs and the panels were made inside, but the assembling was done on the shore when the tide was out. I use to like watching the men tarring the barges, putting the oakum between the joints of the wood panels and the planking. Of course the nailing was all done by hand, and how hard it must have been, hammering nails into hard oak wood. Putting the oakum into the joints was interesting, for they would put a strip along a plank, poking it in hard with a well pointed wooden wedge, when it was far enough to the man's satisfaction, he would tar it, then start packing oakum in again, until no more could be packed in, then it would be tarred all over, so you couldn't see any join. The same was done inside the barge as well, sometimes the man would use an iron rod, with a wedged blade. The operation was called caulking, and the man employed at it was called a caulker. It was a craft continued from the sailing ship days. Another man used to scrape the bottom of the barges and sailing barges. This was called scurfing, and the man who done that operation was called a scurfer. Sparks' also repaired sailing barges.

BARGE YARD OF W.N. SPARKS & SONS.   *(MUSEUM OF LONDON)*

Formerly occupied by Surridge & Hartnoll and subsequently by the lighterage firm of W.J.Woodward-Fisher Ltd. Taken in about 1938, the photograph shows sailing barges moored up for repair. The sheeted structure on the far right was one of the chutes for loading rubbish into barges from the former Stepney Borough yard at Duke Shore Wharf.

When I was a boy, we used to call the River Police 'Water Rats'. Why, I don't know, but it was an old nick name. They were a common sight on the river, chugging along in their open motor boat, engine in the middle of the craft. There was a long wooden seat along both sides of the boat, a coil of rope on top of the wooden engine cover, made of mahogany, the steering wheel was in the middle of the boat, so with the steersman, five men were in each boat, but I have seen only three men sometimes. These craft went up and down the Thames, in heavy rain, sunshine or snow, night and day, during the 1914-1918 War, and in foggy weather.

MAIN ROADS AND RAILWAYS

Limehouse was a busy parish when I was young, and I well remember what went on. Besides the river and canals being busy, so was the Commercial Road, with horse traffic, one and two horse drawn vans or carts were the usual thing. But if they had heavy loads, they would have three or four horses to pull them along; especially the long, low trolleys, on the back of which I use to ride, with other children, as they were easy to get on. It was a common thing to run behind carts and jump on. Of course some carmen would flick their whips at you to get off.

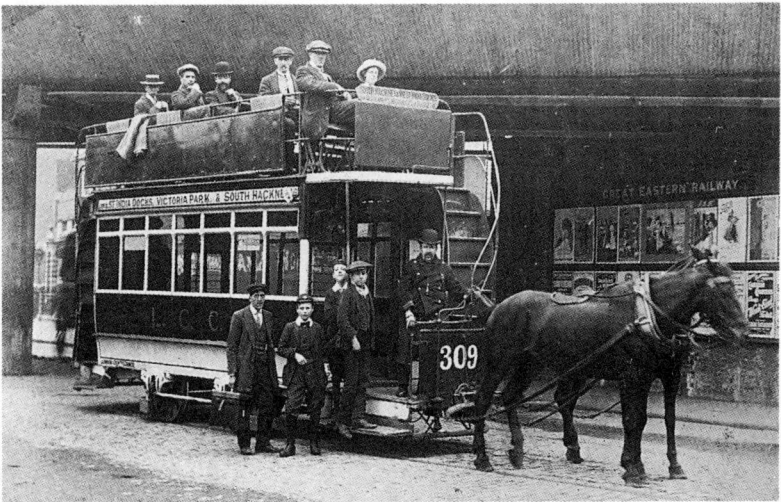

THE LAST HORSE TRAM TO VICTORIA PARK & SOUTH HACKNEY   (ISLAND HISTORY TRUST)

The last horse tram north of the Thames about to make its final journey from the terminus in West India Dock Road, by the London & Blackwall Railway bridge - the horses having just been requisitioned by the Army in August 1914.

My earliest journey that I remember, was to Victoria Park by horse tram, along Burdett Road. The tram depot was then in West India Dock Road, on the left side, near the dock entrance. The fire station was also near there.

How the trams used to jolt and swing from one side to the other, when riding on the top, and more so when they had electric trams, for they went fast. The electric trams also ran along the middle of the road, where you took the risk of oncoming traffic to get

8

on them. The inside tram seats were along each side, and were slatted. How the old tram driver used to ring his bell, when he was held up by the traffic! The bell push was on the floor near his feet. There was also a horse bus, which went round Millwall. The driver collected his fares by putting his hand through the roof of the bus, and holding up a tin. In this tin you put your fare, as there wasn't any conductor. Also the driver wouldn't start until he had collected all the fares before he set off. But later on, Commercial Road had petrol buses, open on top. The back rests were slatted to let the rain water off, and the seats had a thin leather apron to put over your legs when it rained. The London & General Omnibus owned them. They had hard rubber tyres and long seats inside, upholstered.

Another journey, that one of my sisters took me on a couple of times, was on a train from Harrow Lane, a turning off High Street Poplar. From there the train took you to Greenwich Subway in Millwall. On alighting there, my sister would take me and my brother through the subway, to Greenwich. Sometimes we stayed in the Island Gardens, which were on the river front, before we went home. Sometimes we went back by train, but mostly we walked home, because we didn't have enough money to ride.

Millwall was a busy place then, especially during the weekdays. For there was a lot of ship repairing done by some of the big repair firms, such as Green & Silley Weir, Harland & Wolf and the London Graving Dock. There was Mortons, the food preserving people, whose big warehouses employed hundreds of women and girls, and a lot of men too. There were other big warehouses besides the big engineering firms, who employed hundreds of men, so at 'knocking off' time, thousands of men and women would all be coming home at the same time, from both the Poplar and Limehouse end.

Something else connected with transport, were the roads which were cobble-stoned except outside the Hospitals, Churches, schools, and big houses, such as in Burdett Road and East India Dock Road. These had wooden blocks laid down, sprayed with tar over them, and in between them. This was for quietness, as the cobble stones of granite made such a noise, when the steel banded wheels of the horse and carts, and the horses with their iron shoes ran over them. After the road blocks had been laid down a good long time, the rain used to get to them, and they would swell with wet, causing a big bump to come up in the road, so up would come the blocks, and new ones relaid. The strong smell of boiling tar, as it was boiled up and spread over the blocks, and the excitement of poor people and children, to get the old blocks to burn on their fires, for some people had to have fires all the year round, as they had no gas laid on.

9

Burdett Road had a lot of big houses, some of which are still standing at the Limehouse end. When I was young, before and during the 1914-1918 War, I have seen servants and maids in some of these houses, and a coach and horse waiting in front of them. Property was well looked after especially private property. It was a common sight to see the painters in the summer, patiently working away. First with a blow lamp, burning the old paint off, then filling in the cracks with putty. The undercoats were either white or pink, for two coats were put on before the top coat went on. The graining, which was very fascinating to watch, was done with different types of metal combs, which had either fine or wide teeth. Nearly all street doors were grained, and the panelling in the passages was grained as well, besides the varnishing, which was put on all good woodwork. Some stone work was grained, like marble, even that was varnished.

HORSES, PONIES AND DONKEYS

The horse drawn brewers' drays, horse drawn coal carts, bakers' vans, cartage vans, moving vans, funeral hearses and carriages, nearly all transport was horsedrawn, but there were a lot of steam waggons that pulled heavy loads long distances, and the noise they made puffing along the street! Dust carts were horse drawn, so was the water cart, which let a spray of water out behind, and boys used to run behind in the summer, with their trousers rolled up, no boots, and getting the spray on their legs. The police vans or Black Marias, were horse drawn. The doctor would visit in a cab or growler, as it was called, and the ambulance was horse drawn.

One of the bakers who came round the streets was Prices, who had a horse and tip-up cart with two big wheels, these were thin spoked, well painted and varnished like the cart. The horse was well groomed, and the harness shining bright. The baker's vanman was a smart man, who wore a suit and highly polished gaiters. His legs must have ached when he finished his round, for he had to step up into the van every time he had to get a loaf for a customer. He also had a basket for bread. A long rod of iron stretched down from the front of the cart, with a flat plate of iron attached to it, this was about five inches square. The baker stepped onto this, and brought his other foot up to put on an iron plate attached to the rear end of the shaft, so as to get the bread out of the van. Sometimes the baker came round with a small van or box on wheels, which he pulled along himself. At night the vans were lit with oil lamps, which were made of brass.

The funeral horses used to have a tall black feather on their heads, and a mauve velvet blanket or pall on their backs, which hung a few feet from the ground. They were black Spanish horses. There were a few hansom cabs, and the rank was at the Eastern public house. All cabs no taxis. Also there were no petrol coaches to take you on a day's outing or beano, instead there were horse drawn brakes where you mounted from the back, with two long upholstered seats, each side of the long carriage. The coachwork was highly polished and the back rest was neatly carved rosewood or mahogany. The carriage was all open, except for a canvas canopy which was rolled back if very fine weather. I saw one of these, used for a ladies' outing at the Brunswick Chapel, which was in Three Colt Street. The other was from the Britannia public house, which was opposite Limehouse Town Hall, and is now a garage. This was a shipwrights' outing, on shipwrights' day, when they had the day off.

The donkey pulling his barrow was another usual type of transport. In fact I have seen many a man pulling or pushing one too, for they were really hand barrows. The donkey could be obstinate at times, but he worked hard pulling his load around the street. Many a mile he had done before he was put in his stable or shed at night. The ponies worked in a similar way.

In the winter evenings, the barrows, pony carts, horse carts, pony traps, hand barrows and box tricycles were all dimly lit by paraffin lamps, which were square in shape, but they also had a red glassed hurricane lamp at the back of the carts, in fact all vehicles had a red rear lamp of some sort. The bicycle had a paraffin or acetylene lamp. The acetylene lamp gave a bright white light, but could be dangerous when being filled.

11

CARMEN AND WEIGHBRIDGES

If a carman worked for a good transport or carrier firm, he was lucky to be protected from bad weather, such as snow and rain, as the seat where he sat, or dickey as it was mostly called, had a covering which consisted of a flat or round board above the carman's head, fixed by two iron rods stretching from the back seat. Some had the back seat boarded in, some had a board down each side. The seat could not be all covered in at the sides, for the carman had to put his arm out to let other traffic know he was going round a corner.

The driver of a good firm had a good weatherproof peaked hat, an oilskin coat, so long it nearly reached down to his ankles, also an oilskin apron, to go over his knees. These were all supplied by the good carrier firms, such as Carter Patersons, and the various railway companies.

On some of the windows on coffee shops near the river and docks were the letters L.C.T.U. which meant, London Carmen's Trade Union. Why the letters were on the window I don't know, but there were a lot of coffee shops by the river and docks, and not all had letters on their windows.

BROTHER COOK *(MR. HARRY COOK)*

F.B.Cook was a carman with James Watson & Sons of Emmett Street and was presented with this sash by the London Carmen's Trade Union in 1911. The Cooks – all ten of them – lived downstairs at 70 Gill Street, which was demolished for Padstow House.

Branch Road, leading from Medland Street to Commercial Road was always called Horseferry Road by people when I was young. In fact the name was up on the stable wall of the big coal and fuel dealers called Sergeant Longstaff & Co. The stables projected well out on the Medland Street side, opposite Medland Hall, making the roadway very narrow, so that the wheels of a horse and cart touched the kerbstones of both sides of the short bit of roadway. The coal firm got their fuel from barges and coastal ships.

A common sight outside a big firm, if they had a big front yard, was the sign 'Public Weighbridge', and the amount they could weigh up to. Abbotts in Burdett Road had one, which weighed up to thirty tons, just inside the gates, big enough to take a big cart, in fact I've seen motor vehicles weighed on them. The name of the makers and where the weighbridge was made was stamped on them, and some had the date when they were made. There was generally a little office in front of the weighbridge, and a lever bar connected from the weighbridge to a bar balance scales in the office. There was a special name for the scales, but I only knew them as the weighbridge scales, and I knew the little office as the weighbridge office, because I worked at the Limehouse Paperboard Mills where they had one. The cart would be weighed first, if empty, then weighed again going out with its load on, or weighed with a load on, and then again when unloaded.

HORSE TROUGHS
AND COFFEE STALLS

There used to be a lot of horse troughs and drinking fountains for people. I well remember the metal drinking cups attached to a metal chain, and drinking from them. At the bottom of the troughs was a part chipped out to hold water for dogs. There was also a brass tap at one end to fill buckets of water.

THE EDINBURGH CASTLE   (BARNARDO'S)

This turn of the century view shows cart horses drinking at the trough outside what was once a gin palace and music hall which Dr. Barnardo bought in 1876, and converted into his main centre for mission and social work in the locality. The site in Rhodeswell Road is now the car park for the East London Stadium.

In Commercial Road at the corner of Lowell Street, underneath the Railway arch, there is a drinking fountain for people made of red and grey marble, and attached to it at the bottom in granite is a drinking recess to hold water for dogs. This was erected as a memorial to Thomas and Daniel Barrett of Stepney Gate, Three Colt Street, Limehouse, by their sister in 1886. There was a granite horse trough by the kerb in front of it, now taken away, like the one opposite on the south side of Commercial Road, also taken away. Another horse trough was at the top of Salmon Lane, outside the leather and harness shop, now both gone.

Some drinking fountains for people had a block of stone in front for children to stand on, so they could reach the brass press button

14

which let the water from the tap.

When there were a lot of coffee stalls about, they were always near a horses trough, the reason for this was that they got their supply of clean water from a tap at the end of the trough, with which they made the tea in the big tea urns. A tap was attached to the tea urn from which they poured the tea. Some used big kettles. All were on a coal fire stove.

Some of these coffee stalls were out all night as well as all day, and closed only on Sundays and Holidays. Most of their lighting was by paraffin lamps, some acetylene lamps. The big kettles to hold the boiling water to make the tea were made of cast iron, and were very heavy to hold, especially when filled with water, so they were mostly tilted over to pour water into the enamel or tin tea pot. All stalls were on wheels, to be moved about, the coffee stall holder sold tea, coffee, cocoa, bacon sandwiches, sausage, ham, meat dripping, corned beef, fish paste, brawn, breakfast roll. All between two thick slices of bread and well buttered. Toast, which you could have with butter, dripping or fish paste on it, or egg. Even egg sandwiches, boiled hard, and sliced, or soft fried egg on one slice, the same with fried bacon. Some sold Siedlitz powders, a very good remedy if you felt unwell, or if you got drunk, they soon sobered you up the next morning. They also sold Beechams pills.

Market stalls were lit with paraffin flare lamps. Some they pumped air into, and they were able to use gas mantles on them, so that they gave a bright gas light. Other stalls used ordinary household lamps, or candles. At Christmas I have seen some market stalls illuminated by Chinese paper lanterns. Policemen on night duty would have lamps attached to their belts, behind them.

DUSTMEN

It was a common sight and sound to see and hear the old dust carts, with their iron rimmed wheels rumbling by, and the clippity clop of the horses' iron or steel shoes against the hard granite stoned road. Their dull lit oil lamps reflecting into the bedroom window, while I was laying in bed at 11.00 p.m. There was the tired carman's "Gee-up there!" or "Get along there!" So tired. There would be about twenty or more carts, from the market clearings, all going back to the dustyard and depot at Duke Shore Wharf in Narrow Street. The old dustcarts were like a light brown coloured box, with a ladder hooked on behind, and a couple of galvanized baths, a broom, and a couple of shovels.

When they started emptying the street dustbins, the ladder would be put in position for the dustman to climb up the cart. He would lift the dustbin, swing it across his shoulder, climb the ladder, then tip the rubbish into the dust cart. Four men were employed doing this, some dustbins being too heavy to lift, his mate would help him. Sometimes a householder would have more than a binfull of refuse, especially the shop keepers, so that was the reason for the shovels and baths.

As they went along the streets, the dustmen would be shouting out "Dustman!" The horses were ever so patient, stopping and starting all the time. The carts were washed down in the Narrow Street depot, where the rubbish was loaded onto barges and sailing barges. The rubbish dumping was moved to a new depot the other side of Regent's Dock Bridge when they started using motor vehicles, the big Borough Garage was being built at the same time.

The dustmen wore a head covering of leather, with a piece of canvas attached to it, which hung down partly covering the neck. The jacket had pieces of leather sewn on the shoulders, so that the dustbins didn't hurt the man's shoulders while resting on them, when he stepped up the ladder. Of course they all wore narrow leather straps below the knees, nicknamed 'kicking straps' or 'fighting irons' The leather shoulder covers and head covering were supplied by the Council. The knee straps were used for climbing ladders or anywhere where knee bending was done, this also applied to diggers and men in the building trade. It came from the Victorian times, when men mostly wore moleskin, canvas duck or corduroy trousers. These materials were thick and stiff, especially the moleskin and canvas duck, the canvas duck was the same as used for making sails.

THREE COLT STREET
AND ROPEMAKERS' FIELDS

Three Colt Street was just coming to its end as a market place, it had several big shops open, and a few stalls. On the corner of Northey Street was a big shipping butcher, Knightbridge's, who also had their own slaughter house, and I have seen droves of sheep and cows go there to be killed, in fact I got lost once, following the sheep which went past our street into another district. I finished up at King David Lane police station Shadwell, where my mother had to come and take me home

Three Colt Street also had big grocery shops, a china shop, a German butchers, Edward Balls, who also had his own slaughter house. Fruit and green grocers' shops, sweet and clothes shops, such as men's outfitters, where my stiff collars were bought, and a ladies dress shop on the corner of Gun Lane, after called Grenade Street. The stalls were fish and green grocery stalls, outside their own shops, three bakers, one was a Justice of the Peace, Mr. Marks, the other two were Germans. It also had about five pubs and an oil shop and chemist. Plenty of traffic went through it to get to the wharves along the river, Millwall and the docks.

THREE COLT STREET.
(ROYAL COMMISSION ON THE HISTORICAL MONUMENTS OF ENGLAND)

Looking south in about 1910 towards the Old King's Head on the corner of Narrow Street, still standing today. The weatherboarded shops were opposite the junction with Ropemakers' Fields, a bakers handcart stands outside Siebert's, one of two German bakers in the street.

A lot of coastal boats that came to the Aberdeen and Dundee Wharves, carried passengers who went through Three Colt Street to get to Limehouse Railway Station, which took them to the City, or to East India Dock Road, and boys and men used to run up to them saying "Carry yer bag guvner", or "missus", whatever the sex may have been. Plenty of City workers used Limehouse Station and at hopping time it used to be busy with the hop pickers and fruit pickers at fruit picking time, which took them to Fenchurch Street Station, and on to London Bridge Station, to go to the hop fields or fruit picking in Kent.

A FENCHURCH STREET TO BLACKWALL TRAIN ARRIVING AT LIMEHOUSE.
LINE DRAWING BY J.E.CONNOR.

From 1840 right up to closure in 1926, the passenger trains on this line ran every fifteen minutes, taking only seven minutes from Fenchurch Street to Limehouse Station in Three Colt Street and then eight minutes to Blackwall.

In Ropemakers' Fields (a street from Brightlingsea Place to Three Colt St.) was a blacksmith and ropemaker who employed schoolboys to help make the ropes and ship's rope fenders. I didn't work there but I used to watch the smith banging red hot iron on the anvil. Further back was the Black Horse pub, and in between the pub and smithy was a little general shop, which was very small and had a bow fronted window. At the top of the street was a Welsh dairy, where they kept their cows and sold milk and dairy produce. They employed men and boys to go round the streets selling their milk, pushing a wheel barrow, which had a big brass churn from which they got their milk, putting it into small pewter milk cans. The rattle of the cans, as they pushed the milk float over the cobbled stones, and the cry of "Milk!". They also had a bigger float which was drawn by a horse, and I can hear the cloppity clop as the horse was urged into a fast trot and the rattle of the milk cans over the cobbles.

18

NARROW STREET

Narrow Street like its name was very narrow, and at places, only one horse and cart could get by. So at Duke Shore, where Sanders the big corn chandlers had their big warehouses, they used to load up their vans with the result that all the other traffic was held up until loaded. The river used to come more inland, where the old Borough Yard was, and opposite bales of hay were stored, so sometimes you walked under the bowsprits of the sailing barges as the hay was being unloaded.

NARROW STREET
E.W. Taylor & Co. (Forwarding Ltd)

Looking east from Duke Shore Wharf in July 1934 before the buildings on the left were demolished for street widening, this side is now part of Ropemakers' Fields Park. Whilst the building with the anchor still stand on Anchor Wharf, a few of the other buildings on the right, including the old entrance to Duke Shore Wharf, have made way for residential development.

Sanders Brothers were corn chandlers and seed merchants. They had a chain of shops nearly all over London, they sold dried fruit, haricot beans, dried peas, brown sugar and oats of different kinds. Their firm stretched from Ropemakers' Fields to the water side, where barges were loaded and unloaded with their merchandise. Besides having their own horses and carts, they also had their own steam wagons, so they employed a lot of men, besides the women to mend and make their sacks.

Also in Narrow Street there were two or more mast and oar makers, one named White, the other named Lamb, many a time

I have watched them. Also Sparks' the barge builder and repairer and Etheredge's the tug repairers and engineers. Barnett's were marine tackle and rope dealers, afterwards Philips took over the business.

Next to the Grapes public house was the Harbour Master's house, it may have been Victorian or possibly Georgian, as it was bow shaped at the back with two verandahs, one on the ground floor, the other on the first floor with an ornamental iron balustrade. From the ground floor verandah, a flight of wooden steps led down to the river the same as the Grapes had. During the 1914-1918 War it was used as a hospital, and many a time while playing on the river shore near the Harbour Master's house, I have seen wounded soldiers in their blue uniforms sitting out on the verandah.

THE HARBOUR MASTER'S AND THE GRAPES.

(LONDON BOROUGH OF TOWER HAMLETS)

From 1857 to about 1911 this was the residence of the officer responsible for shipping in the Lower Pool. The Grapes, like so many Limehouse pubs once belonged to Taylor Walker's the local brewery. It now forms the end of a row of listed buildings which extends from Duke Shore Stairs.

Inside was a wide staircase which started at the street door, on the left side of the house, and went round the room touching three walls. The wide doorway was Adam design, like some of the other doorways of the shops or houses which were along there, going towards Kidney Stairs, where there was a coffee shop in the old David & Harp pub, owned by Morrows, whose brother had the ship's mast and oar makers business in Brightlingsea Place, where I lived, opposite the Grapes pub.

20

The Grapes public house, a very old pub, had wooden stairs at the back leading down to the river. This pub was mentioned by Dickens, I think in 'Our Mutual Friend'. I think it was built in the seventeen hundreds. In the little saloon bar on the counter was a gas lighter, for the men to light their pipes with. It was in the shape of an old fashioned sailor, who wore a straw hat with a ribbon around it, a striped blue and white jersey, wide blue trousers and made as if he were doing the hornpipe. The gaslight came out of his pipe.

NARROW STREET
(GREATER LONDON RECORD OFFICE)

Taken in about 1920 by William Whiffen, the well known Poplar photographer, this picture shows the bridge over the street which was built soon after the opening of the Stepney Borough Council's Power Station in 1909. It conveyed coal from Blyth's Wharf to the furnaces which raised steam from river water. The Harbour Master's House next to the Grapes and other buildings beyond were pulled down in 1923 to extend the wharf, now a terrace of luxury townhouses.

BRIGHTLINGSEA PLACE

The house we lived in in Brightlingsea Place was made into two flats. There were four houses, all built the same in the 1890's. One had no gas laid on, as gas piping was not put in when the four houses were first built. We went up one wooden step when entering the street door, the door itself being solid beech, no letter box, and a solid iron door knocker, and big iron door knob. There were two locks, one, a big old fashioned iron lock broke, and the other was a modern spring lock.

In the ground floor flat there was a bedroom on the right of the passage, next to the bedroom door was a flight of narrow stairs to the upstairs flat. The living room door faced the street door, this room had a stove with an oven. The oven had a cast iron shelf in the middle, round in shape, with holes making a pattern, and at the same time letting heat through to the top compartment. Ovens were very good for baking cakes, bread and roasting a joint of meat in them. The stove also had a small round iron plate on a swivel, which we swung round in front of the fire to put the iron on, when my mother done her ironing. There was also a grid below the firebars, which we pulled out to put a kettle of water on, or a saucepan of soup to get hot in front of the fire. All the cooking utensils were of cast iron, so when they were full of liquid, they were heavy to put on or take off the stove or hob as my mother called it. Even the frying pan was heavy, being made of cast iron. In the living room were two cupboards, one went under the stairs for coal, the other cupboard was for clothes etc. Next to it on the left, next to the fireplace, was the dresser and cupboard. Over the fire was a mantelshelf and gaslight. In the middle of the wall next to the window was a door to the kitchen, which had a brick built copper for washing in it. Next to this was a fireplace with a mantelshelf, a cupboard in the next wall and a sink and water tap in the corner, then a window and the yard door, no gaslight. The toilet was in the yard, which was 'L' shaped.

Going up to the upstairs flat, the living room was on the left of the stairs and the bedroom was on the right. The bedroom had a Victorian fireplace, the same as downstairs, and a small hearth and small mantelpiece. The fireplace projecting out caused two recesses. The one near the door to the room helped the door to open wide, the other recess gave room for a small armchair. There were two windows looking on to the street, a bed was put against the blank wall, the next wall had a shallow cupboard over the well of the stairs.

Inside the living room was a fireplace with a fire range like in the downstairs flat. There was gaslight over the fireplace. The gaslight in the bedrooms of both flats was in the centre of the ceiling. In the wall opposite the entrance was the door next to the kitchen, then a window overlooking the back yard. Next to the living room entrance door was a cupboard, which backed on to the cupboard in the bedroom.

On entering the kitchen the brick built copper was on the right in the corner, next was a fireplace, not a cooking range like in the living room, but it had a round swivel trivet. An iron gas stove was next to the fireplace. On the next wall was a cupboard, unable to open wide, owing to the gas stove. Then next to the cupboard was a toilet, having a little window to let the light in, and a wide wooden seat and galvanised tank. On the next wall was a shallow sink with a water tap, then a two foot space to the door wall.

My mother paid 7/6d old money a week rent for the upstairs flat, but 10/- of old money when she moved into the downstairs flat, as we had a back yard. My mother must have moved into the upstairs flat in 1910 or 1912, I well remember the 1914-1918 War started while living in the upstairs flat.

I think the name of the owners of the flats was Fielders, who had a lot of property in the East End of London, like their relations who were the Banks. Fielders had a firm to manage their property, such as doing house repairs and collecting the rent. The name of our rent collector was Mr. Flint, and he lived in St. Leonard Road, Poplar, Bromley-by-Bow end. He called for the rent regularly every Monday morning at 10.00am, rain sunshine or snow. He didn't have a bike either.

While we were living in Brightlingsea Place, my brother Sid went camping with his scout troop in 1911, where he caught a fever. He was taken in a horse drawn fever cart to the fever hospital. My mother was not allowed to go with him in the conveyance, but had to go to the hospital to fetch him home. He was in there three weeks. In the meantime, our living room was sealed off, as that was where he had been laying when ill, also the kitchen was sealed off. This was done by shutting the room door tight, and sticking long strips of newspaper down between door and frame to stop the sulphur fumes from escaping. The sulphur fumes were made by burning sulphur candles in the room.

Consumption was a common illness when I was young, especially among young teenagers. These and others in their twenties got T.B. as it was commonly called then. It was terrible to see them suffer.

When we were living in Brightlingsea Place, the man downstairs had consumption, and he always sat on the doorstep when the weather was fine, winter and summer, so when we had to go into the street, we had to squeeze past him. He was a very tall man, over six foot tall, and very nice, not complaining once. His wife was as tall as him, and they had a son who died of consumption. The mother died of cancer in her seventies.

The two men who drove the Sentinel steam wagons lived next door to where I lived in Brightlingsea Place. Many a time they brought them in front of the house before going on a long journey. What a noise they made, as they stopped them and started them off again, letting off steam and shaking the ashes out, then dropping the ashpan to empty the ashes, which were always left in a pile near the kerb.

One of the drivers was called Mr. Smith. He was married and had one daughter who died in her teens from consumption. He lived downstairs. Upstairs lived Mr. Kemshall, the other steam wagon driver, who came from a small country village like his wife, and both spoke with a real proper country brogue. They had two children a girl and a boy. Both men drove the wagons during the 1914–1918 War and into the early 1920's.

In Brightlingsea Place when Morrows the ship mast and oar makers had an order to make a mast, they had to make it in the street, as their building was not long enough to make it inside. So many a time I have seen the street littered with wood shavings and the oar makers busy, carving away at the mast. The main tools they used were the adze and the spokeshave, and what an accurate eye they had, when using the adze. A few strokes down the oar or mast of a ship and it soon took shape, being finished off with a spokeshave. Of course they began from a full tree trunk complete with bark. The masts they made were for sailing ships, steamships, sailing barges and skiffs. The oars were for barges and rowing boats, I forgot sailing yacht masts and flag masts and poles. The bargemen and lightermen used a hitcher or barge pole. This tool was a pointed spear and half way down had a piece of the metal cut out to form a hook. This was fitted onto a pole which the oar and mastmaker made. He also made the wooden blocks for the barge's pump. Except for the ship masts, all other work was made indoors and in winter the main lighting was gaslight. The big chips of wood from the mast and oars they sold to the people for 1d a bag, or, if a woman wanted a pennyworth, she held out her coarse apron and got it filled up. These women used it on wash days, to boil the water up in the copper, which was in the wash house.

CHIVERS COURT AND WILLOW ROW

In the street where I lived was a little private house owned by a little old lady who wore a mauve bustle dress if ever she went out. In her little back garden, she grew a grape vine which produced bunches of grapes every year. The horses' stables of Sanders Bros. were next to her house and we heard the horses quite plainly when restless. Our house backed on to a square and a couple of houses that faced it must have been built early in the 18th century. They were three floors tall, plus cellar, three of them together and the outside ones had feather boards instead of a brick wall down to the first floor. Another house had the bottom of the street door separate from the top half, and all houses had three steps to the street door, owing to the Thames flooding, which it did once, when many people were drowned in Westminster. Our own house was flooded as well, it occured during the night in 1928. These houses were in Chivers Court, at the end of which was a wall of Taylor Walker's brewery, a big firm that employed many people.

Many of the houses had paraffin lamps for light in winter, some in my street, though we had gas, yet the electric power station was in the street. Some of the houses in Chivers Court had no water laid on, besides no gas, and they got their water from a tap in the court. There was another lot of little cottages who got their water from a courtyard, Willow Row, which also had a copper, and the cottagers took turns to do their washing. Many a time, coming or going to school, I have seen clouds of steam coming from the courtyard as some woman would be doing her washing, even on very cold days, and when raining.

The cottages had one room upstairs and one down, ever so small, and you entered from the street into the living room. The community around there was mostly Catholic and Irish, and many a time the very old Irish women used to sit on the kerb or their doorstep, some on a stool, and they would sing all the old Irish songs, some you could not understand, as they sang in the Irish language. They lived in the little cottages.

CLOTHES

Women all wore skirts and clothes down to their ankles when I was young, and some clothes dragged on the ground. Girls wore long frocks well below the knee, white cotton pinafores, black woollen or cotton stockings and either boots or shoes, the boots were buttoned up at the side. Some, like the boys, had no shoes and went around barefooted. A lot of women wore shawls over their shoulders when going shopping, or if they stood at the door gossiping, and some even indoors when cold. The lady in the house where I lived wore one, and when she went to work (sack mending by hand) she wore a shawl, a man's cap on her head, with a hat pin through it, and a skirt down to the ground. Some of these shawls were of heavy wool, sepia brown and white pattern, and must have cost a lot to buy, others were black, light in weight, and looked cheap, as some were going green, both were fringed.

The women inmates at Southern Grove and Poplar Workhouses wore pure white aprons, a black shawl or sometimes a cape done up with a button at the top, frock or skirt and blouse, and on their head a little bonnet. They wore strapped shoes fastened with a round shoe button. As a little side line of their own they made various articles and on Sunday morning a woman would come round and knock at the door and ask if you wanted to buy an iron or kettle holder, women's small aprons, dusters and children's bibs. Sometimes men came round, they wore a cap, thick jacket and trousers and boots.

Most elderly women wore a cape and bonnet, some of elegant design. The cape would be of black material, tied by two ribbons at the top, and decorated with small beads, made into a floral pattern or other designs. The bonnets of black straw would be decorated with pink or red flowers, and green leaves as well, some also with little flowers. These flowers took a lot of patience and time to make, though some girls and women could be very quick at it, but their pay was very small. The women and girls who put the beads on the capes were also very low paid, but had to be quick and had to have very deft fingers, but the women who wore them always looked very nice and smart, in fact the bonnets were quite cute.

Elderly men wore an old cap, a spotted scarf either dark blue or red, a dark jacket, and either a pair of moleskin or brown corduroy trousers, and heavy boots, hobnailed, and handkerchiefs, if they had one, red with white spots. Boys wore caps, a jacket and jersey knickers done up with two buttons at the knee, some without, woollen turnover socks or stockings, and lace up boots which could be hobnailed, some boys wore clogs, which had wooden soles and heels, and leather uppers. That was in winter, in summer they ran about barefooted. If some boys fathers were in regular work, they had a blue serge suit, a stiff white collar and bow tie.

A lot of schoolboys wore Norfolk Suits and small peaked caps, which we nick named 'pimple hats' as the cap had a button on the top in the middle. The button was covered in the same material as the hat, the hat being round and small. The Norfolk suits were made of a tweed material, and the trousers going just over the knees and done up with two buttons. The jacket had two pockets and a top fob pocket, also a half belt at the back. My brother and I wore grey flannel knickers, sometimes of tweed, and a woollen jersey with two buttons on the shoulder, which we undone to take off, shoes, sometimes boots, mostly in winter, and turn down socks.

Well dressed men wore spats in the winter made of felt or cloth with white or black buttons up the side of them, which were done up with a button hook. These spats went over the top of a man's boots or shoes to stop the mud splashes. Elderly big business men wore grey topper hats, a gold tie pin, a silver or gold top walking stick, a gold watch chain and also a long tailed jacket. I have seen many working men such as foremen, shipwrights and craftsmen with a thick solid gold watch chain, with a gold watch attached in their waistcoat pocket. Most foremen and well dressed working men used to wear a blue wool serge suit, cheap serge suits were not all wool, and they were thin, and soon got shiny.

SHOPPING

There were a lot of pawnshops and moneylenders about, but poor people would rather go to a pawnshop than the money lender, as the money lender used to charge 1 penny for every shilling borrowed or one shilling in every pound, some charged two shillings, and one shilling for each week that you could not pay it back.

MONDAY MORNING AT FISH'S PAWNSHOP.

(TOPHAM)

House wives with bundles outside the Pledge Department in Heath Street (now Head Street) photographed by John Topham in the Thirties. G.S.Fish, Jeweller and Pawnbroker of 541 Commercial Road, was established in 1863 and ceased trading in 1983, when the interior of the Pledge Department was removed for reconstruction in the Ragged School Museum.

The farthing coin was much in use then, and I bought many a farthing's worth of sweets when I was a boy. The tradesman priced his goods with the farthing, such as $2\frac{1}{4}$d or three farthings each. The halfpenny was in common use as well. Bread was $2\frac{1}{2}$d a loaf, and a bag of flour or 'half quartern' was $1\frac{1}{2}$d, sugar was $1\frac{1}{2}$d a pound, and tea 6d for a quarter of a pound, coal was two shillings a hundredweight and some was £1 or £1.10s.0d a ton. You could get 14lb of coal or $1\frac{1}{2}$d bucket of coke, and $\frac{1}{4}$d bundle of wood.

When you bought a loaf, it was sometimes underweight, for the bakers always weighed the loaf before they sold it to you. So if the loaf was underweight, he gave you a piece of bread pudding. When I was a kid, I often thought it great, although it wasn't a very big piece of pudding. I've often thought since how unfair it was of the bakers. Why didn't they replace the shortage of bread with a slice of bread, or reduce the price of the loaf, as there were some big poor families in those days.

Coming back to things being so leisurely, of a summer evening women would go and do a bit of shopping, for shops were open until 8.00pm of an evening, some even later. As some men's work was casual, they were paid daily, especially dockers, so some women had to wait until their husbands came home before they could buy anything, and that is when they would go round to the corner grocer and get 1d or 2d worth of jam, and a 1d packet of tea, $\frac{1}{2}$lb of sugar and $2\frac{1}{2}$d tin of condensed milk. The 1d or 2d worth of jam was taken from a brown stone jar by a wooden spoon and put in a saucer which the woman or child brought to put it in.

Others would go farther afield, and would stop on the way to talk to a neighbour or friend who may be sitting at their door. I have known Northey Street in the summer when nearly every house had someone at the door, a lodger might be at the window looking out, or talking to some women, and girls would be at the door or sitting on the window sill knitting or crocheting, and the beautiful things they used to make! This applied to other streets as well.

THE ICE CREAM SELLER OUTSIDE THE FREEMASONS' ARMS

(LONDON BOROUGH OF TOWER HAMLETS)

ODD JOBS AND HOBBIES

Besides babies' clothes mens socks etc., that were knitted, some women and teenage girls crocheted mantel borders. These used to go on the mantel piece to make it look nice, which it did, as they hung down from the mantel piece, some over two feet long. They had different patterns, and all one colour, of red, blue, green, amber and many other colours. Some had silk ribbon thread through them, and nearly all had fringes and tassels. A lot of women and girls used to make their own clothes besides altering them to the latest fashion. For nearly all women's books had a paper pattern inside already cut out and marked, to whatever size they wanted. Lo, behold when your sister or another female took it into her head to make a new dress or blouse, there would be the paper pattern spread out, pins and material all over the place, and then the whirr, whirr of the sewing machine, if they could afford one, otherwise it would be stitched together by hand, which I have seen done many times. Also there was the darning of socks and woollens.

The patching and mending of clothes or alteration of them, was often done at the street door, or back yard in the summer. As to men, their odd jobs or hobbies were indoors or in the back yard. Back yards mostly had a fowl house and six or seven fowls, some more if the yard or back garden was big, most small yards only had rabbits.

Then some back yards had an aviary, where the men, or their sons went in for pigeon racing, what fine prizes a lot of them won, cups and certificates. A lot of money, time and skill was spent making aviaries, fowl and pigeon sheds. Some breeds of fowl that were kept were, Leghorns, Wyandotes, Orpingtons, Rhode Island Reds, not forgetting Bantams. Pigeons were of the racing type and the aviaries held a mixture of linnets, canaries, chaffinches etc. Then besides the aviaries, birds were bred indoors as well, especially canaries. But sorry to say most birds kept indoors in small wooden cages were largely English birds which they kept for their songs, as some birds' notes sound beautiful, such as thrushes, linnets, chaffinches, blackbirds and others. Most people who lived in apartments had one of these birds kept in small square wooden cages, the length of each side being five inches, and six inches high, the front having wire bars to give it air.

One of the cruel things or pastimes when I was a boy, was when men used to take their birds in their small cages to a beer shop, where they held competitions to find the bird that sang the best, or kept his note the longest, and to make matters worse, the cages were covered in a black handkerchief, this was so the poor bird would not know night from day. These bird competitions were held around Limehouse Fields near Stepney Church, and outside the 'Jug House' in Aston Street, Thank God this has all been done away with.

At the end of St. Paul's Road, where it joined Rhodeswell Road, there was a triangle of grassland, and in the centre was a tree, with wide spread boughs and a circle seat around its trunk, where people were able to sit on hot sunny days. The grassland was nicknamed 'Goats Common', as men used to bring their goats there to feed on the grass. I only saw one brought there when I was a boy, but a lady who lived around Limehouse Fields when she was young, said her father told her there used to be lots of goats on it at one time. I believe this as a lot of back yards had goats, and I often saw boys and men taking a goat along the street. A family in Northey Street kept one.

One of the men's jobs at home was boot mending, for though there were a lot of boot menders about in Limehouse, most men liked to mend their own to save money, so it was a common sound to hear boots being mended, women's footwear as well.

It was also common to see boys and men with a penknife, chipping away at a piece of wood making small boats, first the hull, then the mast. Also stamp boxes, book marks, stamp books, needle books, even small boat oars. I saw a wooden chair done by penknife once. I always carried a penknife and done a lot of whittling as it is called, but I wasn't very good at it.

One of the pastimes among young men, some married men as well, was fretwork. They bought a book called 'Hobbies', and in it was a folded sheet of paper, with a pattern in green ink printed on it, of a piece of furniture, such as an art pot stand, over mantels, wall cabinets, stools, screens (fire and door), small tables and many small items such as trinket boxes, letter racks etc., which used small pieces of wood left over from the bigger jobs. The paper pattern would be fixed to the piece of wood they were to cut out, and away they would go merrily, with their fretsaws, cutting out the pattern, following it with great care. Some men used a foot treadle machine if they made many big pieces, also if they wanted to do more than one piece at a time, they would put two or three on top of one another. I have seen some very nice pieces of furniture and bric-a-brac made on a fret saw machine and by hand, which I know some people would like to have in their homes today. Mat or hearth rug making was another popular hobby with men and women, and sometimes the whole family. They would get a good potato sack or a strong piece of sacking, cut the sack down to two lengths of a hearthrug, then they would get all the strong pieces of material from men's and women's coats, women's skirts, men's trousers, cut the material in two inch strips then lengths of four inches, and with a special hook, draw each piece through the sacking in rows, but making a pattern with the different coloured material. The children would be cutting the material into strips and then short pieces, the parents would put the pieces into the sacking. When finished these rugs and mats looked smart and warm, and many poor homes had them.

HOUSEWORK AND FURNISHINGS

As you see people took great interest in their houses if they could, if they were poor they kept them very clean and bright, even the old tin lamp in some homes. Their time was well occupied, scrubbing floors, doorsteps, dusting, for there was a lot more furniture and articles in the home than they have today. As for the washing, everything had to be boiled, then scrubbed with a scrubbing brush, on a scrubbing board. Then the ironing was done by a hand iron, which was put on a good bright coal fire or on a gas ring if you had gas.

Nearly all houses had a boot or shoe scraper which was mostly on the right hand side of the street door, and built into the wall. Some of these were very ornamental and artistically made, having figure heads and patterns of flowers and fruit on them. Halfway down was the scraper, a straight bar about two inches wide. A lot of householders took pride in their boot scraper, for the metal was well black leaded. The well or hole in the wall was where the boot or shoe went through to be dragged back, pressing the sole of the boot on the sharp edge of the scraper, causing the mud to be scraped off. The walls of the well were nice and white, having been whitened over with a splash of whitening, which was used for whitening the door step or the fire hearth, when it was needed.

Many men had longer working hours and had to do harder work in those days, so many a man came home bodily tired and was glad to put his feet up when he got home. Some men worked to 6.00pm and 7.00pm, and to 1.00pm on Saturday. I have worked to 1.00pm on Saturdays myself, 48 hours a week. Then a lot of men worked overtime as well to earn more money. Of course some homes were well furnished and the quality and style was very good. A good chenille or velvet table cloth, well fringed, on a mahogany round table, good ornaments with cut glass drops hanging from them, that glittered like diamonds, the same as the glass on the top of the chest of drawers, which was mostly cut glass. My home had a chest with the top full of cut glass, and the brilliant colours that glistened from it when the sun shone on it. The stuffed birds under glass domes was another common ornament in most homes, some tall, others short.

If you went in some houses, especially in the parlour or front room, it would be so packed out with furniture that you had to squeeze round the table if three or four of you went in, for besides the big round table, there would be six chairs, the fire place furniture, of a big brass or steel fender, tongs and poker, the fender sticking well out into the room. Strange to say I very seldom saw a fireguard in the parlour, but always there was one in the living room.

A LIMEHOUSE LIVING ROOM IN 1912   *(LONDON BOROUGH OF TOWER HAMLETS)*

The mantel shelf was packed with small ornaments, photographs and clocks, that's besides the big ornaments with glass drops at each end, or the stuffed birds in the glass cases. The walls would be packed with pictures or photographs, and a good home had a piano, so the top of it would be full of photos. Over the mantel

33

there were sometimes little shelves with ornaments, and by the window would be the plant stand with the aspidistra plant in a nice big china art pot. Some art pot stands were well made, in mahogany, walnut, oak or ebony, and some had hand carved decorations on them. Some art pots were very elegant things, being decorated with a country scene, or flowers, some were hand painted, some had two handles, some were without any handles, if it were a good one, it would be made of fine china.

OUTDOOR PASTIMES

After Sunday dinner a lot of people visited relations or went to bed 'till tea time, the children playing in the street or going for walks.I have seen a neighbour go to another who could not read, and read the newspaper to them, for a lot of people could not read, especially the elder ones. This was done at the street door in the summer where a lot of people passed the time away, sitting on the step on a chair, on a week night as well as Sundays if it was fine. Teenage girls and boys would get a big rope and have a skip. I have seen as many as thirty skipping and taking turns at the rope. For a joke I have seen men and women in their 30's and 40's having a skip. Though people were poor they got enjoyment out of life. Lots of skipping was done on Easter Sunday, and I have seen grown up girls or teenagers going round from street to street with a skipping rope, and people took it for granted when they saw them skipping along.

In the evenings or afternoon in summer chaps and girls would get together and have a sing song. They would start with the latest and modern songs and finish up with very old ballads, even the school songs, and some had very good voices, which made it sound very nice. Sometimes they were accompanied by a couple of mouth organs for a lot of boys could play them, even some men, which caused them to have a dance, such as the cake walk, waltzes, one step and ragtime. Then on Saturday, if a barrel organ played outside a pub at closing time, I have seen men and women doing a knees up or the cake walk, as many as twenty or thirty of them dancing together.

Another pastime on Sunday morning for a lot of people was to stand on the jetty by Regent's Dock entrance, for a lot of craft were up and down the Thames on Sunday owing to the tide, and such a lot of ships using the Thames, even a lot of foreign boats.

There was always something to see of interest on the Thames causing it to be full of life. Some barges would be towed by a tug, some tugs pulling as many as ten or eleven barges. But a tug sank once pulling too many barges, so they made a law that a tug should only pull six barges at one time. A tug sank near Stepney Power Station with all hands on board once.

There used to be young ladies and women among those at the jetty, and some men used to take their children for a Sunday walk, while their mums were cooking dinner. There used to be a lot of openings to the river and steps so that the lightermen or men who worked on the river could get to their craft. They reached them by rowing boats rowed by a man who got a living rowing men to different craft, or rowing you across the river. I have been taken across the river, also up and down the river by my uncle, who owned a rowing boat. Buses did not run through the Rotherhithe Tunnel then, so to get to the London or Surrey Commercial Docks, or if a lot of Limehouse men wanted to go across the river, they hired a rowing boat.

Rotherhithe Tunnel had little boys who wore a black peaked uniform hat, red jacket, black trousers and highly polished boots. These boys were employed collecting the dung that the horses left behind. There were a lot of boys employed at one time, as a lot of horse drawn traffic used the tunnel, both northbound and southbound. The boys were smart and well behaved, and must have been orphans. I might be wrong, but the boys may have come from Dr. Barnardo's Home a big orphanage where there were a lot of children, both girls and boys.

Some of the boats I remember in Regent's Dock being unloaded were the ice boats. The big blocks of ice that were unloaded went to the butchers, ice cream makers and fish shops. The big dock warehouse by Branch Road was not built then. Facing Branch Road, but in Medland Street was Medland Hall, and I have seen a long queue of beggars and tramps queuing from Medland Street to nearly the top of Branch Road for a meal of soup and bread.

REGENT'S CANAL DOCK

(ROYAL COMMISSION ON THE HISTORICAL MONUMENTS OF ENGLAND)

This 1905 view from the ship lock shows three-masted barques from Scandinavia with cargoes of ice and timber and steam colliers from the North-East unloading coal into barges, mainly for the gas works along the canal.

A few people who lived close by used to sit by Kidney Stairs. But the most popular place was Limehouse Pier. Crowds of people used to get there in the summer, for it had a floating pier which went well out into the river, so as the tide rose, so the pier rose with it, and was connected to a bridge which half rose with the tide when it came up as well. On land was a pub so people could have a drink of beer and watch the boats go by, for there was a low wall which you could sit on. Besides barges, tugs and sailing barges that used to come to the pier, sometimes they had pleasure boats which used to collect passengers or disembarked them. A lot of boys used to swim there, and I just remember when they had the greasy pole and a bit of a water carnival. The greasy pole was an old ship's mast which was smothered in grease, and hanging from it on short bits of string were toffee apples. Well, boys had to try and climb along the greasy pole and try to get the toffee apples which very seldom they were able to do, for they mostly slipped into the water, much to the onlookers' delight, and causing lots of laughter.

LIMEHOUSE PIER:THE FOOTBRIDGE & GANGWAY.   *(GREATER LONDON RECORD OFFICE)*

Built by the L.C.C. in 1905 for the penny paddle steamer service on the River Thames, but trains and trams were preferred, especially in the winter, and the service was scrapped in 1907. This 1908 photograph from the pier at low tide shows the gangway and the footbridge by the Horns & Chequers pub, with watermen's skiffs laid up after the opening of the Rotherhithe Tunnel.

LIMEHOUSE PIER, VIEW TAKEN FROM THE RIVER AROUND 1914

(LONDON BOROUGH OF TOWER HAMLETS)

CUSTOMS

There were a lot of old customs kept up when I was young. The earliest one I remember was 'Jack O' the Green'. There was a canvas tent the width of a man's umbrella, dome shaped at the top, the tent about six feet tall, gaily striped with ribbons hanging from it in different colours. A man was inside it, twisting it around causing the ribbons to flutter out. Outside was a man dressed like a country dancer with bells round his knees which jingled when he danced about, and he held a gaily ribboned stick in his hand which he waved about, shouting all the time. There was another man with a dirty sooty face, dressed in old clothes and a high topper hat, holding a witch's birch broom, and a couple of boys in ragged clothes and sooty faces all calling out or sometimes singing. I was afraid of them, and used to run away, but I have found out since that it was the chimney sweeps on the first of May. They also carried branches with leaves still on them.

May Day was made a fuss of by the carmen, who used to deck their horses out with gay paper flowers, attached to their harness. The leather straps of the harness used to be well blackened, shining brilliantly, the same as the brasses and buckles, all well polished and shining brilliantly. On the mane over the forehead would be a short bow of ribbon, sometimes two, and the tail would be plaited with coloured ribbons. If the tail were short, there was a bow of ribbon. The flowers were between the manes, though there were always two or three brasses hanging between them. Some horses would have a straw hat on, if fine weather, and with its ears poking out from it, it looked really funny, though gay. The carman would have a flower in his lapel buttonhole, and a bow of ribbon on his whip. It was a common sight to see a flower in the lapel buttonhole of a man's suit, especially the rose or carnation in the city businessman's suit, or teacher's. But it was surprising the different variety of flowers the working or poorer man wore. For many men having their own little gardens, it's surprising what they grew. Also flowers were cheap to buy. For 6d you got a nice bunch of flowers, daffodils and wallflowers were only 1d or 2d a bunch. In fact some roses were only 2d each, so that was why they were worn every day.

Seeing the old year out and the new year in was a happy noisy time. I remember being taken to Regent's Dock Bridge, Narrow Street. As soon as it struck twelve o'clock, then the noise and excitement began, ships hooters would start hooting, coloured flares rockets and fireworks would go off. A lot of people would be banging anything that made a noise. Crowds of people would be there, all singing 'Auld Lang Syne', or 'The Miner's Dream of Home'. There were a lot of ships on the river then, besides those in Regent's Dock. A lot of foreign ships were amongst them, which gave the foreign sailors a chance to let themselves go. A lot of men and women started dancing as they got drunk, but I can't forget the loud ringing of church bells, the same as on Christmas morning. The enjoyment lasted over half an hour. When we came away, all would be shouting, "Happy New Year everybody!" Then a lot of people being superstitious, the darkest person would go indoors first, carrying a piece of coal for luck, and some carrying salt, what the salt was for, I don't know.

We used to have a lot of very thick fogs when I was young. We could only see a few yards with some fogs. They were a thick yellowy colour. I remember Trafalgar Day, they made a big fuss of it then and it was mostly a very foggy day. Fog caused a lot of noise on the river as well, for if there was a high tide, a lot of craft wanted to use it either to get up or down the river, so you could always tell it was a big boat by the loud long moan of the ship's horn, or the tug's short sharp hoot, and the ringing of the tug's bell. There used to be a fog horn going as well.

CHILDRENS GAMES

The different games we used to play in the streets I thoroughly enjoyed. Tippet was one. It was like cricket, only the two batsmen had sticks, and had a piece of wood, eight inches long instead of a ball to hit. The stick had to be in the centre of a chalked ring, until you struck at the tippet. The pitch was only six feet long. If your tippet was caught, you were out. If one of the opposing team saw that your bat was not in the ring, he would shout "tippet!". Two of the opposing team would then take the tippet, go away, and come back with the tippet hidden on one of them, they would each go to a batsman who had a chance of getting a score by putting his stick in the other's ring, or the tippet being put in his ring. If the tippet got in first the batsman was out.

Buttons was another game. You got some good strong buttons, such as soldiers' brass, or livery suit buttons, it was best to play with about four boys. You would bounce the button against a wall and see how far the button would go out. Then the boy whose button went out the farthest claimed all the buttons. If two buttons were level you spanned with your hand from you opponent's to yours, if you couldn't reach he would try, if he could reach, he got your button. Buttons went by numbers, that is the amount of spans the button went out after hitting the wall, some went up to twelve, but the common or usual ones were four or eight.

Grottoes used to be made up on Saturday, two pieces of bright wrapping or shelf paper would be put up against a wall about two feet high from the ground, in a tent shape. In the opening would be an ornament, mostly a figure, or sometimes a candle. Some had picture postcards, or pictures cut out from books on the wall. A coloured piece of paper was laid in front of the tent-like pieces, held down by sea shells, bottles with paper flowers in them, or some decorative article. Then as the people went by, the children who made the grotto would run up to them saying, "Don't forget the grotto, please don't forget the grotto". This was a girls' pastime, and a girl would always be minding somebody's child, if not her own baby brother or sister while doing it.

NARROW STREET   *(TOPHAM)*

This Thirties photograph by John Topham looks west, with Old Sun Wharf on the left and the entrance to Noah's Ark Alley on the right, where the Stepney Borough Garage was built in 1938. Old Sun Wharf is now a yard for Tower Hamlets refuse vehicles whilst the other riverside warehouses have been converted to residential use.

BRUNSWICK CHAPEL
AND EPPING FOREST

When I was very young, that's before the 1914-1918 War, my sister Grace used to take my brother Sam and myself to the Brunswick Chapel at certain times of year, near Christmas and in the summer, either June, July or August. The reason being that the people who were in charge of the Chapel, one being the Reverend Mr. Rowe, gave out a white paper bag, and in it was an orange, apple, piece of cake, sometimes a piece of bread pudding, and always with some boiled sweets, such as winter mixtures. That was at Christmas time.

In the summer we went to Loughton in Epping Forest by train, either from Burdett Road Station, or from Stepney Station. On reaching Loughton, we were taken to the Retreat, which had a lot of wooden tables and forms. Here we were given a white paper bag which contained a meat pie, some bread and butter sandwiches, and a cake or a piece of cake.

The week before we had the winter bag, and a week before the day's outing at Loughton, we were given a round ticket about three inches wide, and a piece of thin string threadled through it, and on it was printed 'Ragged School', 'children' might have been printed on it as well, but I forget now. But it was a good sight to see a long trail of children in the summer, walking to either station, with their pale blue round Ragged School ticket hanging from their jersey or jacket if a boy, or their dress if a girl. And what a long walk it seemed when a toddler, going from Loughton Station to the Retreat, for there were many toddlers who went, both girls and boys, who were looked after by an elder sister.

Our time was occupied by games such as sack races, three-legged races, races for different ages etc., prizes were given to the winner, such as sweets, a religious tract story, books and games such as Ludo, Snakes and Ladders. We could also go for a walk into the Forest, by following a man who held a banner up high. Sometimes a big boy would hold one up at the back of the file, on these banners in big words was 'Ragged School'. Hundreds of children went to Loughton from Brunswick Chapel, and a special train was put on for them alone.

It cost one half penny to go to the Brunswick Chapel for the children, which was on every Thursday evening at 7.00pm, and only children could attend. First you said a prayer. Then you sung some hymns, which were being played on a big piped organ. The two hymns I remember most were, 'Pull for the Shore Sailor, Pull for the Shore', and 'Yes Jesus loves me, the Bible tells me so'. While the children sang, there were pictures being shown on a screen, projected from a magic lantern, which had a chubby faced child leaning on its elbows. The other was a lot of men in sou'westers pulling in a lifeboat. Sometimes we saw a movie picture which was very flickery, and you couldn't see properly for a minute when the lights went up. There was also a short session of children saying a piece of poetry, and singing a hymn, for which they got a book prize.

It was a big building and had a fine organ, which was played loudly when the kids sang the hymns loudly. It used to get packed with kids, so you can guess what a noise was made. My sister always took us up to the gallery, as there was so much talking, shouting and babble by the children that we hardly heard the girl or boy say their poetry or sing their song, until one of them in charge shouted as loud as he could, "Quiet Children!" The third shout would be heard well, and then there would be dead silence and you could hardly hear a pin drop.

How we loved going there, we queued up outside, down a court at the side of the Chapel, and when it was time to go, there was one big crush to get through the small doorway. A lot of children got their clothes torn, I did too. Sitting inside the doorway was a man at a table to take your halfpenny.

My last visit to the Brunswick Chapel was during the 1914-1918 War, but I was surprised when my eldest sister, when she was eighty five years old, told me how much she used to enjoy going to the Brunswick Chapel when she was a girl.

After the 1914-1918 War was over they started the Ragged School outings again to Loughton, and it was from Northey Street School where I was a pupil, that I went. We went from Stepney Station, marching along the Commercial Road with the Ragged School ticket hanging from our jackets. One long line of girls first, and then a long line of boys following. The teachers being in attendance to keep us in order. Our time was taken up with cricket, races and tug-of-war, but there were no prizes.

CINEMAS AND THEATRES

The first moving film I saw was of a man being chased, who kept falling over and tripping over things. I thought it very funny, and there were roars of laughter from the children. The other picture was a sad one with a woman holding a little girl's hand going through the snow. This was at the Brunswick Chapel, and they charged ½d to go in. The next moving picture I went to see, was at a little cinema in the High Street Poplar, called the Star, and it also cost ½d to go in. I saw John Bunny, Pearl White and a lot of big stars of them days. We used to see two comics, two dramas and slides about what was being shown the next week. The other cinemas I was taken to by my youngest sister, these were the Kinema, or Fleapit (its nickname) in Whitehorse Street, also the Ben Hur in Whitehorse Street.

Whitehorse Street was a busy market then, near the Church, and nicknamed the 'Old Road'. The other cinema was the Majestic, which was in a cul de sac and near a school in Ben Jonson Road.

I remember people reading aloud in the days of the silent films. In them days a lot of people, especially the elderly, couldn't read or write owing to little schooling or bad eyesight. So while you would be looking at the picture being shown, as soon as the captions or wording came on someone would read it aloud to the person they were with. It might be a man reading to his wife, or vice versa, or a couple of women, or some woman would have one of her kids read to her. So there was always a good deal of mumbling going on and if the cinema wasn't too packed, you kept away from them. Jews done a lot of this reading aloud, for there were a lot of Russian, Polish and German Jews in the East End who couldn't read or speak English.

Another thing at the Ben Hur cinema was women doing their potato peeling, during the 1914-1918 War and on until the late 1920's. The 'Old Road' was a very cheap market, so what some women used to do, was to do their bit of shopping just before 2 o'clock, then queue up at Ben Hur's which opened at 2 o'clock. While watching the films the women would peel their spuds or when the film changing was on, for the lights would go up then. So the cleaners, besides nut shells and orange peelings to clear up, had potato peelings as well, some women peeled carrots, swedes and parsnips as well.

A very common sight was women peeling potatos outside a public house, there was always a long wooden bench outside some pubs in the summer, like the Young Prince in Chrisp Street. A woman would meet another in Chrisp Street market and have a little chat, then one would say "I do fancy a drink", and off they would go to the Young Prince where other women they knew were outside. So they would get their drink and all start talking to one another, and if they had bought their vegetables and had a big family, out would come the spuds and, borrowing a knife from the publican, start peeling away whilst talking.

Sometimes I was taken to a theatre. One was in High Street Poplar, called the Queen's. The other was the Poplar Hippodrome in East India Dock Road, at the corner of Stainsby Road. There never was any cinemas or theatres in Limehouse. I have seen some big stars at them both and I saw Charlie Chaplin at one of them before he went to America, and the last big star I saw at the Queen's was Harry Secombe, though I saw Gracie Fields in the revue called 'Mr. Tower of London' many times at the Queen's Theatre. Marie LLoyd, Kate Carney, Little Tich, G.H.Elliot and a lot more stars of their time I have seen at the Hippodrome. About 1925 it was turned into a cinema and it was badly bombed in the 1939-1945 War.

My sister Nora took me to Drury Lane Theatre, I took a tram to Leman Street, where she used to work. On meeting her, she would take me by bus to Wellington Street. At Christmas time she took me to the Lyceum Theatre to see a pantomime. One pantomime I distinctly remember was Cinderella. What beautiful scenes there were in some of the acts! When Cinderella came on in her coach it was breathtaking to me, as it was all illuminated by electric lights, and drawn by real live ponies! I can still remember it, as plain as anything now, also the singing and ballet dancing was magnificent, especially as little girls as well as big girls danced on their toes.

The Poplar Hippodrome used to have some very nice pantomimes at Christmas time, and the local shop keepers and publicans in Limehouse used to get a fund up to help the poor children of Limehouse to see these pantomimes at the Poplar Hippodrome every Christmas time. Also the children of the regular customers at the grocers, butchers and other shops got a ticket, so as to draw custom. So, as my mother was a good customer and bought a lot of groceries at C.Gore, I got a ticket, and was able to see some pantomimes. Besides having two shows in the evening, they also had a matinee in the afternoon, and it was the matinee the children attended. The whole theatre was filled with children, the stalls. the pit, fauteuils, circle, even the boxes, but not the gallery. So through these free outings, I was able to say I have been in every part of the seating accommodation of a theatre, and I was also able to see some good pantomimes.

The Queen's Theatre in Poplar High Street also had pantomimes at Christmas time. What a fine frontage the Poplar Hippodrome had! With its mahogany and glass doors, highly polished including the big brass door handles, and the wide fancy shaped brass plates at the bottom of the door which stopped them from being damaged, and the wide marble step. These were all highly polished and cleaned by three or four women every morning. The thick red patterned carpet that covered the foyer floor, and the plain red carpet on the stairs to the circle, these were edged with wide canvas strips to stop the carpet curling up. Even the canvas strips were daily whitened. There was the tall military commissionaire outside the front of the theatre, who allowed the queue of people to go in at each performance. He was spick and span in his smart blue uniform, highly polished buttons and boots, immaculate white gloves held in his epaulette on the shoulder. There were two uniformed ushers smartly guiding the ticket holders to wherever they wanted to go, and the programme girls in their black dresses and snow white aprons, were all ready to sell you a programme, at 2d each.

Next to the Hippodrome, in the East India Dock Road, were a few shops, and one of these shops was a photographer's who held a competition for the most beautiful actress or chorus girl who would be acting the week the competition was on. The photo of the winner was put in his studio window, and how beautiful some of these girls were!

In Ropemakers' Fields, on the Three Colt Street side of Thomas's Dairy were two little houses which had downstairs windows like shop fronts. In the first one, next to the dairy lived the family named Smith. Next door were the Grooms, a big family of boys and girls. They sold baked peanuts outside the Poplar Hippodrome when it was a theatre. Father sold outside in front of the theatre, Mother went along the gallery queue, both shouting out "Peanuts! Don't forget your peanuts! Penny a bag, peanuts!" Their sons and daughters helped them out when they grew up. The Grooms also went to fairs, such as Blackheath at holiday times, where they sold toffee apples, paper streamers, peanuts and paper fans etc.

THE FIRST WORLD WAR

I distinctly remember my mother receiving my eldest brother's calling up papers. We were in the upstairs front room, when she held the letter in her hand. It was August 1914. Paper boys were running round the streets shouting out "Paper, war declared!", and carrying a bill poster in front of them, with 'War Declared on Germany, Official', and a big bundle of papers under their arms as they ran along selling them. Outside the paper shops there were placards with the latest headlines too.

At the beginning of the War I saw many German Zeppelins at night when the searchlights shone on them and they looked like white cigars. The searchlights flashed on as soon as the Zeppelins were heard, for they made a low moaning rumbling sound like a big dynamo. All the time a Zeppelin was in the grip of the searchlights there was heavy gunfire, easing up only when the Zeppelin dodged the beams. Sometimes, when a Zeppelin was in the grip of a lot of searchlights, we were able to see the British planes flying about the Zeppelin and firing at it. The planes were only the size of ants to us on the ground, the Zeppelin didn't look big either, but when they were hit they automatically nose dived down in flames and everyone cheered, though it was an awesome sight. Sirens used to go off when the enemy were sighted, the same as in the last war, except that at the beginning of the 1914-1918 War a special constable used to come round the streets on a bike blowing a whistle. Sometimes the raid had already started before the special got round, for he had to get the report and permission to give the warning from Limehouse Police Station. It was nearly always a bright moonlit night when the Zeppelins came and people used to say that the Germans could see the River Thames better, so as to follow it up to London. Another yarn was that Crystal Palace being all glass reflected the moon brilliantly so that the Germans knew where they were over London. They painted the Crystal Palace black, later in the War, and all factories with glass roofs and skylights were painted black, even to the factory windows.

I well remember the people raiding and smashing up the German shops, the three German bakers and butcher in Three Colt Street. It must have been awful for the German shop keepers especially as a lot of them had helped the poor people, so my mother told me when I grew up. Though she didn't like the Germans for causing the War, she wouldn't go near the shop raiding.

DURING THE ANTI-GERMAN RIOTS. *(LONDON BOROUGH OF TOWER HAMLETS)*

This photograph from "The Home Front" by Sylvia Pankhurst was taken in May 1915 outside Eliashow Abraham's watchmakers shop at 170 Salmon Lane. It was one of a number of shops on the corner of Commercial Road which was demolished in 1923 for the Empire Memorial Sailors' Hostel.

From the Infants School I passed to the 'big boys' at eight years of age, which was a Catholic Boys' School in St. Anne's Row. It was called 'Our Lady's' after the Catholic Church 'Our Lady Immaculate', which was a small Church then and was behind the house in Commercial Road where the priest resided, the priest was Father Higley.

Our lady Immaculate Catholic School was big and modern, having electric lighting. It was a good solid brick building, with a flat concrete roof, which served as a playground, and I have been up there many a playtime. There was also a playground in front of the school and big glass partitions between the classrooms. The school teachers were strict but they taught thoroughly. The headmaster's name was Mr. Weiler, and our teachers were Mr. Cattrall for drill, Mr. Casey for Standard 4, Mr. Duggon for drawing and two lady teachers, one, Miss Andrews, was my teacher in Standard 2 and taught very thoroughly like the men.

One day in the afternoon, I think it was at play time, when one teacher ran over to another quite excited, and shouted, "Kitchener has been drowned! Lord Kitchener's dead! How awful!", he was terribly upset, for a lot of people liked him. Some placards had 'Kitchener's Dead' printed on them. Others had 'Kitchener Drowned'. Things were looking very black, especially as around where I lived there were a lot of husbands and sons killed, either as soldiers on land or as sailors at sea, and that went on right through the War.

47

MRS. JONES WITH EDITH, ROSIE AND ELEANOR.

MRS. ELEANOR McDUELL Nee JONES)

Mrs. Jones and her six children lived in two upstairs rooms at 1 Cayley Street, next to Knights' Dairy. this photograph was taken in 1916 at Griffith's Studio, Roman Road, to send to Mr. Jones, serving as a private in the Royal Horse Artillery in France, where he was gassed.

The Church was of more importance than it is today, so that more attended either morning or evening at the places of worship. Our Lady's Catholic Church and St. Anne's Limehouse Parish Church both had big congregations. St. Anne's had as many in the evening as at morning, and it had a well attended Sunday School at Limehouse Church Institute in Three Colt Street as well. The Wesleyan Brunswick Chapel had a big congregation as well for the morning service and evening, and in the summer the congregation sang hymns on the chapel steps. Brunswick Chapel also had a well attended Sunday School, morning and afternoon, at the Mitre Chapel, in the little turning called The Mitre between Three Colt Street and Church Row. They also had a cripples' parlour for poor cripple children. My mate, a cripple took me and two more boys. We had hot cocoa and two arrowroot biscuits, sang hymns, and were told a religious tract story. They also held a star class, so called for when you attended you had the card you held stamped with a red star. It was prayer, hymns and a tract story, but no cocoa. We went as it was somewhere to go, and our friends went as well.

The First World War was on at the time when we used to go. Well, while we were being told a story by a Mr. French, there was a terrific big bang and explosion, which sent us all over the place. The big heavy seats fell on us. Some children got hurt, it was a terrible big bang, pandemonium broke out among us children, I faintly remember Mr. French picking himself up where he had been standing on the dais, as he had been knocked over by the explosion. For that is what it was, the Silvertown Explosion. As soon as he could he started shouting, "It's all right children, don't be afraid", for a lot of children ran to the door to get out, but another man was at the door, holding the children back. Well eventually we did get out into the street, the sky was a brilliant red, with reflections from the fires that were blazing, caused by the explosion. Women and men came to get us children, the man in the house came to get us, and there was a lot of shouting and crying, in fact it was chaos. Horses bolted causing a lot of accidents, and there were also a lot of accidents caused in factories where machinery was used. There were fires going all night, a lot of house windows were broken as well.

During the 1914-1918 War, my mother used to go to Limehouse Church Institute, which was in Three Colt Street, at the corner of Batson Street. Batson Street was a half circle in shape, having small houses in it. The other entrance to the street had the Limehouse Railway Station on the corner. My mother used to take me with her sometimes to the Institute, when mothers' meetings were on. Well, once when she took me, Lord Kitchener's sister came and gave a talk to the mothers. Another time a lady police-woman, with the rank of sergeant gave a talk at a meeting. She was very stout, and looked much shorter than she was. This was the first lady police-woman that I ever saw.

I well remember the queuing for different articles of food during the 1914-1918 War, in Salmon Lane, before food rationing became law. The main shops we queued up at, were Coles or Spencers, both fruit and green grocers. News would go around that Coles had some potatoes, people would cause a long queue there as potatoes were so scarce. Coles would be sold out before all had been served, so the rest of the queue would rush round to Spencers before he sold out. My brother and me would start queuing sometimes 8.00am or after as we then had to go to school. So sometimes through queuing we were late for school causing us to get two handers, that was a whack of the cane on each hand. Butter, cheese, sugar and tea were also in short supply causing more queuing at shops such as the Home and Colonial, Peaks, Maypole and Liptons, who sold groceries. One day Maypoles filled their window with saccharine tablets, the tablets were a greeny yellow colour, about half an inch across in size. You put them in your tea instead of sugar, but we didn't use sugar or saccharine.

At the far end of Narrow Street was the Phoenix Biscuits firm, who made the sailors' biscuits, and during the 1914-1918 War they made biscuits for soldiers and sailors. The size of the biscuits was about four inches square and about three tenths of an inch thick. Boys used to hang around the door to be given a broken one, or whole one if they were lucky. I've eaten one many times.

One Saturday morning, while I was sitting on the kerb with two other boys, two aeroplanes came flying across the sky, we were excited, as we had never seen anything go so fast before. Then quite suddenly we heard two terrific bangs, everybody started shouting and screaming: I was told later in the day that they were German Taube aeroplanes, and they had dropped their first bombs on London. In fact they were the first aeroplanes I had ever seen. That same week another of my brothers named Sidney came home from France wounded in the leg, and my elder brother got gassed. We had a continuous two weeks of air raids and bombing. When a bomb dropped on Salmon Lane, at the corner of Copenhagen Street, onto a German bakers shop, a glass partition in school shook violently, causing some panes of glass to fall out on us boys in Standard 2. At the same time Miss Andrews got injured with shrapnel. She was my teacher in Standard 2, but that day went to teach the children in Standard 1. On the same day Upper North Street School, Poplar got bombed, killing and injuring many children, the year was 1917.

We watched the Zeppelin battles at the start of the War, but when the German aeroplanes started to come over and drop bombs it got too dangerous with all the shrapnel flying about. There was a big gun at Blackwall Point which they fired at the aircraft – the noise vibrated nearly everything in Limehouse and Poplar. So people round where I lived ran to the paperboard mill for shelter, but it was too dangerous, so Mr. Hough allowed the people to use his bale warehouse in Narrow Street, near Shoulder of Mutton Alley. The big bales of rags and rope were a good protection and they were stacked high by manpower, though each weighed from twelve to fifteen hundredweight. Of course, us boys climbed among the bales. There were a lot of teenage girls in the shelter, some who worked at Hough's and lived around Three Colt Street, and they used to sing the latest popular songs of the time, such as 'Keep the Home Fires Burning', 'When the Moon Shines Bright on Charlie Chaplin', the parody song from 'Little Redwing' called 'How ya Going to Keep Them Down on the Farm', 'Sargeant Brown Keep an Eye on Tommy for Me', 'Mademoiselle from Armentieres' and 'Parlez Vous'. There were a couple of elderly men there as well, I suppose unfit for the services, and when the heavy gunfire started the men would shout "Come on, sing up all of you." "Come on, louder! louder!" So the men were doing good war work, if not in the services. There was a big pasting machine put in where the shelter was, where they made container boards for boxes.

The Salvation Army Citadel, nearly opposite the Limehouse Town Hall, was another place I liked going to sometimes with my mates, sometimes with my brother. It was held on a Monday or Tuesday evening. A Mrs. Barclay was in charge that evening, her rank was Captain, and the children loved her, and a lot of children went too.

While waiting for the doors to open a shout would go up, "Muvver Barclay is coming!" And a lot of kids would run to meet her, a lot of them would already be with her. She was a short stout person, and would be in her Salvation Army uniform with a long peaked bonnet. She had great patience and a loud strong voice.

We started off with a hymn, "G. double O. D. is Good, G. double O. D. spells Good. I would like to be like Jesus, G. double O. D. Good". Another hymn was, "All Things Bright and Beautiful", the kids sung as loud as they could, in fact they shouted, and Mrs. Barclay would be banging away on the old tambourine, the noise we made! After that we were handed out by child helpers, pieces of cardboard, on them were drawn in pencil thin lines in the shape of animals flowers, toys etc. Along the lines, holes were pierced and through these we pulled a piece of wool threaded in a needle, some holes being so big, we did not want a needle, and followed the shape of the lines made. We also had the wool and cotton reel to pull through to make table mats, some girls done crochet or knitting.

We finished up with a hymn and prayer. Before we started a lot of talking went on, which got very loud, the same while waiting for the wool etc., so Mrs. Barclay had to give a big shout, "Quiet children!" And could she shout? She sure could shout loud! She even spoke loud when talking or preaching, she was a real good character. If married or not I don't know, but I think she lived in Dixon Street In Limehouse.

My brother and I only went a few times, but the next day after the last evening we went, we went to school as usual, marched into the hall to say prayers, which we had a lot of. On going to our classes my brother and I were told to report to the Headmaster who then asked us where we had been the evening before, which he knew of. So when we told him, he told us to bend over a chair, and he gave us four lashes of the cane, as hard as he could. It did hurt. He told us never to go there again, which we did not as my father took us away that week to Wiltshire, as the air raids got so bad. We never told our parents what happened, but I would have liked to know who told the Headmaster, to me that person was proper scum. I had the cane after that, on each hand, and my behind on different occasions and at different schools, but they never hurt as much as St Anne's Row School, Limehouse.

My father took my brother and me to where he had his business at Ludgershall, Andover, Hants, which was then part of Wiltshire. Tidworth was only two miles away, and being on the edge of Salisbury Plain, we saw many soldiers. When they had mock battles in Ludgershall, I used to go and collect the spent cartridges.

From my father's shop in Tidworth Road, we could see the white tents of the camps on Salisbury Plain, and my father had a caravan and tent in Deweys Lane where we lived. From there I used to hear the bugles blown by the bugler night and morning. The bus went once a week into Andover, which was seven miles away, and one train also on Saturday. Collingbourne Wood was quite near, and in the summer we enjoyed walks through it as it was quite abundant in blackberry bushes, nut trees, honeysuckle, oak, sycamore and other trees. Also there was a large variety of different birds, and in winter of lot of these birds used to be in my father's garden.

Most of the regiments in the army then were either foot or horse, so it was a common sight for me to see a long file of soldiers pulling the gun carriages and supply wagons along. While at Ludgershall I saw plenty of Anzac and American soldiers in their uniforms, and a lot of them were very big chaps. There was a lot of practice flying of aeroplanes, some coming over Ludgershall, the aerodromes being at Weyhill, Biggin Hill and on Salisbury Plain. Some airmen were very good, as they done a forward roll or a backward roll, and some as if they were a leaf falling. Also as these planes were frail and made of light wood and canvas, many a wing came off a plane, or the tail would get fixed, which made me see some pilots fall to their death, although some, if their engine stalled, were able to glide down to safety. One plane glided down into a field nearby, so I was able to go right up and touch it. It was a frail thing, being made of wood, also, inside the cockpit were a few clocks, as I thought they were then, on a panel.

These planes could not fly very high, and the cockpits were not covered in, for you could always see if one of two air men were in the cockpit, and many an airman has waved to us as they flew over my father's caravan, and to the children when they flew over the school playground.

The airman that I saw get out of a plane once, wore goggles, a soft helmet which was done up under his chin, a uniform jacket, breeches, puttees and gauntlets. Most soldiers wore puttees, and if they were in the Horse Artillery, they wore stirrups even with their walking out uniform, also a cane. My brother Sid was in the Horse Artillery, and looked very smart in his uniform. My eldest brother was a gunner on the big guns, being in the Royal Artillery as well. A year before the War ended he was released to go as an interpreter at a Lead Mill in Rotherhithe, where a lot of Flemish refugees were employed. My brother was a good linguist, speaking many languages fluently.

While at Ludgershall, my brother Sam and me caught the influenza which was raging very seriously at that time, for many people caught it and died. I had a very high temperature, but had just enough strength to live, it was awful.

BACK HOME AGAIN

After the 1914–1918 War and the Armistice was signed, my father sent my brother and I back to Limehouse again to be with my mother. He got my mother to take us to Northey Street School which we attended until 14 years of age.

When my brother Sam and I were away, we bought a Meccano set number 1.0.0. with our pocket money, given to us by my Dad, and coppers from neighbours if we done a little job for them. When we saved up enough again, we bought another set, number 1.0., we enjoyed playing with them so much we brought them back to Limehouse.

Besides comics we had the 'Children's Newspaper', which my father paid for. This we found very interesting and enjoyed reading it. We bought that in Limehouse, until our newspaper shop stopped selling it.

My mother was strict to make sure we were clean and tidy, especially for school, and one of these jobs of an evening was cleaning our boots with a halfpenny skein of blacking, which was more like dubbing, and was contained in grease proof paper. We had to soften the blacking before applying or using it, so as to make it spread and to do this you either put a little water on the blacking or spat on it, which most people or children did.

One of the toilet soaps we washed with was 'White Swan' floating soap. It was white in colour and had a swan cut out in it, and it used to float on the water. I used to get a piece of wood or matchstick, and a piece of white paper to make a sail, stick the wood in the soap and have a game of boats, especially if there was another bar nearly used up. On Fridays my mother would send me to Wanstalls in High Street Poplar, a big oil shop, and ship's chandlers.

WANSTALL'S IN HIGH STREET POPLAR. *(THE DICKENS HOUSE MUSEUM)*

Taken about 1910, the photograph shows Edward John Wanstall's oil shop, by 1926 it was run by Mrs. Elizabeth Wanstall. The White Horse public house on the left was re-built in the Twenties and is the only building in this photograph still standing today.

At Wanstalls I had to buy 2lb of soda for $1\frac{1}{2}$d, a 2d bar of brown soap, 2 bars for $2\frac{1}{2}$d, a bar of white or blue turtle soap at 3d a bar. This went up to 4d, and then 6d a bar around 1920 - 1921, this was used to wash the best, dainty clothes with, and tallow candles $2\frac{1}{2}$d or 3d each. They were blue in colour with a white centre. My mother said they were made from Russian tallow. Sometimes I got the ordinary white wax candles $\frac{1}{2}$d each or 5d a dozen. I also had to remember to get the green trading stamps given free for every 4d you spent. With the stamps, my mother used to get her cotton lace curtains, pillow cases or kitchen tablecloths. I got soap etc. for Monday, washing day, sometimes to make 4d up I had to get a dozen boxes of matches for $\frac{3}{4}$d or 3 farthings. Sometimes I would get some of the toilet soaps and candles at the oilshop in Three Colt Street. Above the oilshop would be two big oil jars, made out of stone as a shopsign, these were mostly red, green or black in colour.

When I came back to London it seemed so changed, quiet, people not being together so much, in fact people seemed sadder and shaken. It must have been the shock of knowing their husbands and sons would never come back to them again, especially when they saw the other men come home. A lot of single and married men came home wounded. That was a big shock for the men and the women, knowing that they could not take their old jobs on again. Then they found out that a lot of men who were at home and didn't go to war, earned a lot of money. The war being over, men were put out of work in the shipyards. My eldest sister's husband was exempt from war service being a shipwright, but was soon laid off work when the war ended, getting a ship repair job now and again in Millwall. The docks had no armaments to ship causing a lot of dockers to have no jobs, especially as exports were so low. Also women did a lot of men's jobs while the men were at war, so a lot of firms kept the women on. In fact the women didn't want to leave their war-time jobs, as they earned more money, that also caused a lot of men to be out of work. Even my brothers Bill and Sid, like a lot of men who came home from the War, could not get a job until they got taken on at the Limehouse Paperboard Mills. Bill went as a greaser until he went into the Air Force. Sid started as a shoveller, keeping on until he became a machine man and leaving to go as a foreman at another paperboard mill.

THE PEACE PARTY

The big jollification I remember well was the signing of the peace treaty. It was a fortnight of big celebrations. The Union Jack was flown on churches and big buildings, shop windows were full of red white and blue ribbons, and nearly every other street in the East End had a street party. I even saw a party of Jewish children in the Jewish quarter off Commercial Road.

The people around where I lived collected money. Shop keepers gave well in money and sweets. Then they gave us children a big party. It was held in the square at the back of where I lived. They had a ship's mast in the middle of the square, which was given by Morrows the mast makers. It was kept there for a week, with a big Union Jack flying on top.

On the Saturday morning all was excitement and eagerness with the children. Women were hurrying and scurrying getting their shopping and housework done. Then when the men came home from work, and had their dinner, so the fun began. A barrel organ was hired. Mr. Gore, the corner grocer lent his piano, which was dragged from his shop parlour to the square by about ten men. The long tables, borrowed from the nearby beer shops and public houses were laid out with cakes, bread and jam, jellies and fruit, and each child drank their tea from a peace party mug, which they were allowed to keep. I kept my one, but lost it when we got flooded out, when the Thames overflowed a few years later in January 1928.

A gramophone was playing all the time we were having our tea, and someone was standing by to change the records. Women and men kept coming round the tables with a tea pot, cakes, bread and butter and jam, to make sure we had enough. Mr. Gore took photos of different groups of children at the tea, while it was light.

Then, when we had our fill, tables were cleared and put away. Men started to have a drink of beer or ale, and some women as well. The old barrel organ was started up, women and men joking and laughing with one another. Everybody was so happy, children started dressing up, so did some grown ups. Then as it got dark, they took the flag down, and now at the bottom of the mast was an old rowing boat filled with wood from a broken up barge, with tar on some of it, and wood shavings also. When the fire was started, the heat from it was terrific, the mast burnt too. When the fire was alight, people were singing and dancing, the gramophone, piano and barrel organ were playing. Everybody let themselves go. Around the square were strung little coloured glass jars with a candle in each. These jars were about $2\frac{1}{2}$ inches high, and when they were all lit up, they looked very pretty and colourful.

NORTHEY STREET SCHOOL AND ARMISTICE DAY

When I was at Northey Street School they had a boot club which we children paid a penny a week for, and we had a club card to enter our subscription in. When we had the sum of half a crown or 2/6d saved up, our mothers were able to take us to the boot shop to buy a pair of boots for 2/6d. If you could afford it, you saved up to 4/6d for a good pair.

The little boot shop was in Durham Row, a turning off the 'Old Road' Market, or White Horse Street. Durham Row led into Church Passage, on one side the Church grounds, on the other side shops and houses. Church Passage led into Stepney High Street. The boots we bought were hand made, the proprietor was a boot maker.

I'm not quite sure if he made wooden soled clogs, but he sold them, as lots of boys wore them. Two girls who lived in Northey Street wore clogs as well.

Apart from the penny boot club, Northey Street School had a penny bank, we could put in more than a penny if we wanted to. My mother used to put 4d in the boot club, as we wore so many boots out, meaning my brother Sam and I, but she put 2d in the 1d bank, which was drawn out at Christmas and helped us to buy luxuries such as fruit, suet and flour for the Christmas pudding.

One of the school teachers used to take the bank money to the Penny Bank, which was in Commercial Road near St. Mary's and St. Michael's Catholic Church. It was eventually taken over by the Trustee Savings Bank, and then closed down. The name 'Penny Bank' was on the building a long while after being taken over. The building had a two pillared porch, very dilapidated, and still stands today.

the Headmaster at Northey Street School was Mr. Williams, who was my father's teacher when he was at school, and, as I said before, my father paid 1d a week, the same as my mother, to go to school then. My mother went to Wade Street Catholic School, Poplar. The teachers at Northey Street School when I went there were, Mr. Allen, good at science, Mr. Pritchard, a tall man who wore immaculate good suits and always a flower in his fob buttonhole, and Mr. Jehu, a strict teacher who taught well and thoroughly.

CLASS 4 NORTHEY STREET SCHOOL 1923.   *(MR. ROBERT HOWARD-PERKINS)*

On the left is the Headmaster, 'Billy' Williams who became a certificated teacher in 1882 and retired in 1924. Mr. Hardwicke, the class teacher on the right, died in 1926 from gas poisoning in the First World War. Fourth boy from the left on the front row is Victor Higgins, whose father kept the Grapes, and last boy is Robert Perkins.

Empire Day was one of the celebrated days, on the 24th of May. In the morning after playtime, we would assemble around the flag mast, where we would sing the song, "What is the Meaning of Empire Day?", and the Headmaster would give us a talk about the huge Empire which we possessed, and on a platform would be girls dressed in the costumes of each country belonging to the Empire. Then we had the afternoon off from school to celebrate.

Another big event at Northey Street School was the 11th of November, which was Armistice Day in honour of all those killed in the 1914-1918 War. I remember the very first one. It was a cold dull day, and as we waited around the flag mast with the Union Jack at half mast, there was a loud gun fire, a fraction after which there were others, and then complete silence. It was so uncanny to me, those two minutes silence seemed to last for so long I thought they would never end. Then the loud bang of the gun fire let us know that the two minutes were over. Then we began to sing, "Oh Valiant Hearts".

A couple of years later I was in the main road at the time of the two minutes silence, at 11 o'clock. All the traffic came to a standstill, and most of it was horse traffic at that time. People on the pavement all stood still, and as you can guess, the trams and buses also came to a standstill. People stood at their street doors or leaned out of their windows, and some factories let their employees stand at the factory gates. The war memorials in parishes and villages had a good congregation around them, and many beautiful wreaths were laid around them.

The War memorial in Limehouse Church park used to get a big congregation around it on November 11th, and many beautiful wreaths were laid at its foot.

NORTHEY STREET SCHOOL

(MRS. BETTY GOYMER)

Taken with a box camera from the fifth floor balcony of Brightlingsea Buildings, outside number 64, where Clement Atlee lived in 1911. The Board School was opened in 1874, with ground floor classrooms for girls and first floor for boys. The terrace of four houses in the right foreground overlooked the square, where the peace party was held in 1918.

ARMY SURPLUS

After the 1914-1918 War was over, the army surplus stores started buying all the army, navy and air force surplus uniforms and anything of the three services. Also some German articles as well. Now among the British uniforms were uniforms worn by soldiers who were killed by poisonous gas, sent over by the Germans in some of the battles. These uniforms when bought by the surplus stores were sent to Regent's Canal Dock under a galvanized roofed shed, where women were employed to cut off the brass buttons and brass belt fasteners. Then the rest of the uniform was cut up and shredded to be used for roofing felt or respun again to be made into army blankets.

Now the gassed uniforms were supposed to be burnt or completely destroyed on the continent, but somehow, unknowingly, some of the gassed uniforms got mixed up in the ungassed ones. Well one day, there was quite a lot of excitement in Medland Street outside the firm, for there were fire engines, ambulances and a lot of police besides dockers and other people. The excitement was caused when some of the bales of uniforms were opened, poisoned gas leaked from them. Also while women were working on some uniforms, mustard gas was on them causing them to get blistered. So women became ill and sick with the poisoned gas. Men who had opened the bales were affected also. All the dockers at Spurlings Wharf, which totalled hundreds, stopped work until the danger was over. I saw the firemen hosing down the bales and loose uniforms lying around, but I was too late to see any of the victims taken out.

One of the interesting things that came out of Germany was the paper trousers, boots and horses nose bags or chaff bags. The trousers had two paper strips attached, with button holes which acted as braces, buttons were made of wood on the trousers. The boots had paper uppers but wooden soles, the nose bags were all paper. The paper thread was made by narrow strips of strong paper tightly spun into a thread, then woven. I knew one chap who bought a pair of the boots, to wear when he worked on his allotment in dry weather, but how he got on with them I never found out. But the horses' nose bags made good shopping bags, many women bought them, even my mother did, as a vegetable shopping bag, and used it a long time, then as a clothes peg bag.

The boots cost 1/- in old money, which is 5 pence in new, the nose bags were 6d in old money, $2\frac{1}{2}$ new pence. I didn't know the price of the trousers, or anyone who bought a pair, they looked stiff and hard to me. But all three articles were sold in the old Chrisp Street Market and Salmon Lane Market. I was told that they were brought over to England to be pulped into cardboard.

SALMON LANE
AND LIMEHOUSE FIELDS

The Salmon Lane end of Rhodeswell Road led into Copenhagen Place, and in Rhodeswell Road there were two blacksmiths, and one of them belonged to Brights, the horse cart and van builders and repairers. They were an old established firm employing many men mostly skilled craftsmen such as wheelwrights, signwriters, cartwrights, wrought iron craftsmen, leaf spring makers and painters.

Opposite Brights was a little dairy, who at one time kept cows and sold the milk produced from their own cows. They also made butter, the same as Thomas's of Ropemakers' Fields and Abbotts of Grenade Street. When they finished making their own dairy products I couldn't say, but I remember one of the women at Thomas's turning the wheel of the churn to make butter, when I was sent to buy butter, cheese or a loaf of Nevills bread, that was in 1920 or 1921.

The Post Office in Salmon Lane was in a high class men's haberdashery, selling men's socks, ties, collars and gloves, handkerchiefs etc. It was a small shop, owned by a brother and sister whose name was Bell. They were very polite and genteel. Not many people had the 'phone in their house or shop, but some shops had a 'phone box, such as a tobacconist, big paper shops and some pubs, Bells did as well. The idea was to draw trade, and outside the shop that had a 'phone box, was a blue enamel swinging sign over the door saying, 'You may telephone from here'.

Salmon Lane was a busy market when I was a boy, having big shops and stalls on both sides of the street. The Empire Memorial Hostel was not there then, and the shops used to go right round to Commercial Road, one was a cook shop, the other a leather and harness makers, which had all kinds of harness, whips, horses' nose bags that held the chaff that horses ate, and things for the cart as well. How lively and noisy the market was, butchers and stall holders crying out their wares, beggars singing or playing musical instruments, such as a harmonium which had keys just like a piano, but you had to move the pedals with your feet, just like an organ, to top up the air into it. Also there was the barrel organ turned by handle. They played the latest and most popular tunes. Some people used them to sell their song books or sheets costing 2d or 1d, with the latest song in it. A man stood crocheting and some of his work was elaborate, dainty and neat. He was partly blind, and women bought doylies, table cloths and pieces of lace he had made.

Salmon Lane Market began to lose a lot of people when the L.C.C. built the Becontree Estate at Dagenham and whole streets of houses in Limehouse Fields were pulled down by the Stepney Borough Council to build flats. These houses had two or sometimes three families in them because people couldn't afford the rent.

Some old couples only had one room to live in, and when young couples first got married they started off in one room until a baby came along. There was a shortage of houses, also the wages were low, so it was a common thing to go into a mate's house and see a bed or sofa in the living room. If they were very poor, the room would be furnished very meagre and poor. I have been into a friend's house without any oilcloth or linoleum on the floor, perhaps a newspaper to keep the well scrubbed table clean, a sack for a hearth rug and a rope mat in the passage, which had two lines of washing hanging against the wall. On the high mantel shelf would be a couple of tea caddies as ornaments, which held odd bits. Sometimes there would be a fancy shelf paper on the mantel shelf, of pale pink or blue, and with a pattern of flowers, stamped out like lace having a scalloped edge.

I have been in some houses like that and others not so bad. A lot of women wore coarse aprons which were part of a sack. Some women just held them on by a safety pin, but some were made like aprons, and were tied at the back by a bow made from white tape. Some women washed and ironed them, like an ordinary apron, and they did not look bad, but I never saw a woman wear one in the street. On Sunday some women wouldn't even wear them indoors, Sunday was more respected then. People and children wore their best clothes, even the poorest wore something different and cleaned themselves up, and very few people washed clothes on Sunday, in fact it was a proper day of rest.

In Limehouse Fields there were many men in the fish trade, either fish curers with their own fish stall or Billingsgate porters. A lot of men also worked as porters in Spitalfields Fruit and Vegetable Market. One man I knew, used to be a whip minder, as some carmen had very good whips which cost a lot of money, and they could always pawn their whip if they were hard up. A lot of costermongers also lived around there. Then of course there were the men who worked in the docks, mostly casual labourers. A lot of the women from Limehouse Fields worked at Hough's in Narrow Street and London Street, sorting paper, rags, rope and string or in the Copperfield Road factories especially the big tent and canvas firm where the work was very hard and heavy. Most of the people kept pigeons or fowls and rabbits in back yards. Upstairs lodgers all had their geraniums and caged bird on the window sill, even if they only lived in a back room.

It was around this district that bird singing contests went on. Then there were the big card schools and gambling groups, such as 'pitch and toss' and 'up the line'. Sunday morning I've seen six groups around Carr Street near the railway arches, under the arches if raining, Sunday afternoon as well. Of course, there were respectable people and families living around there as well, I've seen many people going through York Road to get a bus in Commercial Road, City way, or a train from Stepney Station, being clerks or in the tailoring and dress making trade.

Barnes Street was where the relief and Council offices were, they issued the free dinner tickets for the children of the poor and the relief tickets for the very poor families. The place where the poor children used to go for their free dinner was in Parnham Street next to Lusty's the turtle soup firm, who used to make the soup for the big function after the Lord Mayor's Show. The dinner meal shop was on a street corner opposite a pub, and next to the pub was a very small undertakers. Mr. and Mrs. Aylward were in charge of the dinners, I was in the same class as their son Thomas , who was called Tom for short. He became a Councillor on the Stepney Borough Council. His sister lived in Gatwick House, where I am writing this, for a few years. When she was a schoolgirl, I think she went to Howrah House, a convent school in East India Dock Road, where they were taught by Catholic Sisters. The schoolgirls wore a blue cup and saucer or mortar board hat.

Parnham Street was a turning off Salmon Lane which had a footbridge over the Regent's Canal. The bridge, up to the early 1930's, was floored with wooden planks and it was called 'the wooden bridge' by people. It became dangerous as wide gaps got between the planks, and it was bouncy, especially when a lot of people were walking on it. When you got over the bridge the first shop on the right was a fruit and greengrocers on the corner of a court of about four houses facing the canal. Next was a cornchandlers, selling poultry food and dog biscuits, a laundry, sweet shop, grocers and I think another fruit and vegetable shop and four smoke holes round the corner.

On the other side, from the bridge there was a cats' meat shop, a bird shop, a bird seed shop - selling various kinds of seed, besides millet in bunches, also various kinds of birdcage, sand and cuttle fish - a bird cage shop and another bird shop on the corner. This side was very popular with a lot of men of all ages, even boys including myself. They were all very small shops, and you went down a step into them. The shop windows had about three shelves, full of bird cages with birds in them of different breeds, as well as those in the shop. Saturday was the busy day.

STREET CRIES

There were many different street tradesmen with their cries. There was the fishmonger shouting, "Fine right haddocks", sounding like, "Figh, ay addicks". The Dutch herring man, crying out, "Dutch herrin's", so sadly. The muffin man, gaily ringing his bell on winter Sunday afternoons in his white apron, with the muffin tray balanced on his head, shouting out "Muffins!" The man selling sprats shouting out, "Sprats alive O". Why "alive O", I don't know. The mussel man crying out so mournfully, "Mussels, 5 farthings a quart", as if he were singing a sad song. There was the fly paper man in the summer, with fly papers shaped like a topper hat on his head full of flies and shouting out gaily, "I've served the Queen, and she's alive, she's alive, fly papers". The knife grinder, calling out, "Scissors and knives to grind, to grind", pushing his old barrow, with the grindstone and a little can of water through the streets, until he got a knife or scissors to grind, and then you would hear his grindstone whirring away as he gaily peddled to make it go round. He would sometimes make a key for you.

There was the whelk man, and on Sunday there was the shrimp and winkle man shouting out, "Fine large shrimps, 2d a pint, winkles". The watercress and celery man, shouting out, "Fine white celery, don't forget your watercresses". But I think the nicest and prettiest street vendors were the violet sellers, who went round the streets singing, "Sweet violets, sweeter than all the roses, sweet violets, nice little posies". Mostly girls and women sold them who were nice looking. The baskets of violets on their arm were strong with scent. The other flower sellers who went round the streets were the man and woman who sold lavender, singing the song, "Won't you buy my sweet lavender". They sang the song right through continuously, and they had nice clear voices, so you heard every word distinctly. A few times about four girls came round selling lavender, and singing the same song as the man and woman.

The French onion man, on his bike, with a string of onions on his shoulder, sometimes walking with his bike, dressed in his dark blue beret, pale blue and white jersey, dark blue trousers, very narrow at the bottom, I never remember the onion man calling out his wares, you beckoned to him.

The cats' meat man was a familiar sight when I was young. He would carry a wicker basket, oval in shape, on his arm, crying out "Cats' meat!", with lots of cats following behind. In the basket would be wooden skewers each with about six pieces of horse meat. Our cats' meat man never called out, as he had a good round and a lot of customers. He charged $\frac{1}{2}$d a skewer, then it went up to 1d in the 1920's.

He also employed a teenage boy to help him.

The window mender, with his wooden crate on his back full of glass, crying out," Any windows to mend, winders". He must have gone home very tired at night, after carrying the weight he did. There was the mat mender, with the coils and balls of coconut fibre string and twine, for most people used to have a lot of coconut fibre mats in their passages, and always there was one at the street door, even if the rest of the passage was carpeted. A lot of men made their own rope mats, and I have seen rope mats with original designs, shapes and sizes, apart from the basic ones. My own father made some very good ones, well designed too.

There was the chair seat mender with his wooden shaped seats well perforated with small round holes, which would be fixed on with either flat headed nails, or rounded brass tacks. Other seats he made were of raffia or string. There was the comic man on Sundays, who used to cry out, "Don't forget your comics", and what a variety he had, besides the weekly novels. From the American cartoon comics, to the English comic cuts, 'Chips' and 'Funny Wonder'. The novels were, 'Yes or No', 'Christian Novel', 'Sunday at Home', 'Pegs Paper' and stories of big murders or crimes such as 'Maria of the Red Barn'.

The salt man was another vendor pulling his barrow through the streets crying out "Salt man!", and now and again he would saw a slice of salt costing 1d, from the big blocks of salt he had in his barrow. Then there was the knocker up man, who woke people up to go to work. You would be lying in bed, when you would hear small granite stones being pelted against the window pane, and a man's deep voice saying, "It's 7 o'clock, and all's well". Winter and summer, rain or sunshine, or snow, he was as regular as could be. Of course he had other times for knocking up, and whenever he called, he told us the time.

The knocker up man had a grocer's shop on the corner of The Mitre and Church Row, His name was Mr. Coles. He knocked us up by throwing small stones at the windows or with dried peas, which he blew through a peashooter.

The paper boys were an exciting lot, shouting out, "Paper, Star paper, big murder, read all about it!", or whatever the front page news was in the papers he sold. There were a lot of different newspapers for sale as well, both evening and daily papers. And it was a common sound to hear newspaper boys shouting out, "Papers!" at 10pm and 11pm at night.

Outside the bakers on the corner of Burdett Road and Commercial Road, was a newspaper stand, where men sold the papers on the pavement near the kerbside, this caused a lot of excitement and confusion at times, especially when there was a big event in sport murder or politics etc. If a boy wanted to earn a few pence for himself, he got it by running round the street selling newspapers, one or two quires. These boys sometimes were barefooted winter and summer, although not all of them, the reason being to help them run faster, also their boots wore out running round the streets. As soon as the newspaper van came from Fleet Street there would be a big dash for the newspapers by men and boys. The newspapers came in big heavy bundles tied with string, these were handled by the men.

KNOCKER UP   (TOPHAM)

Mrs. Mary Smith of Brenton Street, Limehouse Fields. Her customers were usually market workers who had to get up around three in the morning: for sixpence a week, she would shoot dried peas at their bedroom windows. John Topham was a policeman who had been taking photographs in Limehouse for six years when he sold this picture in 1933 to the press and became a professional photographer.

65

RAG & BONE MAN
AND STREET PHOTOGRAPHER

The rag and bone man was a common sight to see, especially during the 1914-1918 War and well up into the 1930's. They bought bottles and jam jars, also they gave $\frac{1}{2}$d for each jam jar, the same for a good bottle. Some men didn't give anything for a bottle, although they took them, and I well remember when they only gave $\frac{1}{4}$d for a jam jar. Some rag men gave crockery in exchange for old rags, such as saucers, cups and plates.

Of course a lot of jam and marmalade was kept in brown stoneware jars, the outside of the jars being corrugated the length of the jar, although not all. Most stone and glass jars had a lip at the top for the string which the grease proof paper top was held on with. The string being white twine.

There were old rag and bone shops also, and these took jars as well. The rag and bone shop in the Chinese Causeway, well away from the Chinese quarter, had a big pair of iron scales, which reached to the ceiling, and iron weights ranging from a quarter of a pound to half hundred weights and hundred weights. The platform of the scales was big enough to take hundred weight bales, as they bought the rags and bones from street barrow men. They sorted clothes of different materials as well, and on some rag shop windows was painted, 'Dealer in old rags, and sorter,' also, 'Dealer in old bones'. People used to buy clothes to wear from them, if they were very poor.

I remember my photograph being taken by the street photographer. Only on bright sunny summer days he came round, carrying his camera on a three legged stand. When he saw a group of women with children, he would stop and have a chat with them. They were mostly refined, well spoken men. Then he would say, "That's a bonny pretty baby", to one of the women, "What a nice photo the baby would make, it's so pretty", so the women would be taken with the child, which would cause some of the other women to have their children taken. The men mostly wore a bowler or straw hat.

Older children's photos were also taken, and when I was young it seemed ever such a long time for him to put the piece of black cloth over his head and get you in focus. Then he would say, "Watch for the dickey bird", unscrew the lens cover, wait a few minutes, then take the piece of black cloth off his head. This was followed by him taking a small piece of tin from the back of the camera and dipping it into a solution held in a round tin hanging from the three legged camera stand. When it was taken out, a photo would be on the tin. It wasn't a good photo, but recognisable and only lasted a few weeks, then faded away.

PAVEMENT ARTISTS
AND SHOP SIGNS

Pavement artists were a common sight when I was a boy. There was one man who used to do crayon drawings along by Limehouse Church railings, a few feet from Limehouse Town Hall. There were not many pictures, about four, but well drawn. But the best pavement pictures were at the Recreation Ground in East India Dock Road. There were about ten pictures to look at. Country scenes, drawings of boats, steam ships, head and shoulders of notable people and Royalty, an angel clinging to rocks with sea waves lashing against them. They were so well drawn and coloured. There would also be a poetical verse in beautiful copy book writing. A cripple sat by the drawings as that was how they earned a living for themselves.

In fact there were a lot of men cripples then. Some with one arm or one leg, one man who hung around the Eastern pub, had both legs off up to his knees, the stumps of legs were in a leather casing, which must have been padded to rest the stumps on. He was able to walk about. Some men had a wooden leg, some a crutch, some had a hook for a hand, some had a big boot. And the amount with only one eye! There were a lot of cripple children about too, but they were mostly deformed from when they were born. The boy next door to where we lived had a deformed foot, his elder brother had half of one of his arms missing. A woman in Chivers Court, had the top part of her mouth missing. The boy with the deformed foot was a friend, and he used to take me and another boy to the Cripples Parlour, which was held once a week at The Mitre. It was packed with crippled children, all with deformed limbs. Some were a bit simple.

Shop signs were common when I was a boy. The chemist in Three Colt Street, like other chemists in those days, had three big bottles in the window, with coloured liquid in them, mostly red, green and mauve. The boot shop and repairer with the big boot hanging outside. The men's hatter with the big top hat and the hosier with the big sock. The optician with the big pair of spectacles hanging outside. The locksmith and tool shop, had a big golden key or a tool of some description that he sold. Many a child would find it a great novelty to see them today, but the children and grownups took them for granted then. The harness maker had a horse's head. I have even seen a well modelled country wagon attached to a fully harnessed shire horse, the modelling was perfect. Of course I never saw that sign in London.

BANDS AND BUSKERS

Of a Sunday in summer it was nice to go to the park and listen to the silver or brass band. Many people went and listened to them, and I well remember the nice bands that used to play in Brickfield Gardens, which was just off Rhodeswell Road. It had a fine big bandstand, and was the only park which had a bandstand in Limehouse. The other park was St. Anne's Church Gardens. St. James' Gardens was a nice park which had a band playing in it on a Wednesday evening, but there was no bandstand, only a dais, and they allowed dancing when the band played. It was a pleasant park, having plenty of trees, and well kept lawns. One part in front of Bekesbourne Buildings was a flower gardens, where only adults were allowed to go, no children, unless accompanied by an adult. In fact only babies were allowed, because they wouldn't make a noise or touch the flowers. The flowers they grew there were magnificent, and in a large variety of different colours, not forgetting the roses and other flowers, which threw out such a beautiful scent. I spent many an hour there in my teens after which I would go on an afternoon shift of 2.00pm - 10.00pm. I have been there on Sunday evening and listened to the hymns sung by the congregation in the old church of St. James', and as it got dusk, to see the coloured glass window, which was lit up by the church lights.

St. Anne's Church Limehouse had a beautiful coloured window and looked magnificent when lit up of a Winter Sunday evening. The sound of the congregation singing so well and sounding so nice, is a beautiful memory to me now. So the parish of Limehouse had its beauty and places where you could go and avoid the Chinese Causeway or Pennyfields. Pennyfields was in Poplar, and not in Limehouse as a lot of people thought.

In the 1920's the People's Palace had free concerts on Sunday afternoon, until it was altered into a theatre. The artists being highly talented pianists, singers, harpists etc. The Scouts had good shows to raise money for troop funds, and to hear the Scouts band being played as the Scouts marched smartly through Three Colt Street from Brunswick Chapel to The Mitre was a fine sight and sound, especially as the band played for about twenty minutes in front of the chapel. I think it was on the first Sunday of each month.

The Salvation Army Bands caused a lot of people to congregate and listen to their fine playing, especially when they played a popular modern tune to a hymn, which would be outside the East India Dock gates on Sunday evening. A group in Northey Street had a fine lot of bandsmen. The Salvation lassies had the old fashioned poke bonnets then and sounded ever so fine when they sang alone, gently tapping their tambourines now and again, and the band playing softly in the background. There used to be a big band outside the Sailors' Palace, the top of West India Dock Road, sometimes having a conductor and a concertina to accompany the choir. It was a fine sight and sound when they marched back to their place of worship opposite Limehouse Church in Commercial Road.

The buskers, not all, were quite good entertainment. One couple, a husband and wife, sang outside pubs, both had good strong voices and it was quite entertaining listening to them. In fact when they were young, people used to stop and listen to them. The husband had one eye and played on the harmonium, which he carried on his shoulder from pub to pub. He must have been very tired when they went home. They sang all modern songs, and you could understand every word they sang, so you soon learnt the words of a new song from them.

A man who rattled two spoons on his leg, playing a mouth organ at the same time was worth listening to, especially as he vamped so well on the mouth organ. Another man played a pair of clapper bones in each hand, giving his hands a rest by singing a song. He had a good voice and sang very well.

The old tin whistle blower was a common sight and sound outside a pub door, some of them made a good tune on them. A lot of street organs were about, outside pubs in market places, and streets where a lot of people passed by, some sold modern song books, increasing their sales by a man or young chap with a good voice singing one of the songs out of the song book. One man used to play a dulcimer very well, the instrument being so well tuned that you enjoyed listening to it.

ERNEST STREET BARREL ORGAN
DEPOT   (TOPHAM)

From about 1913 to 1940, this depot was run by an Italian, known as 'Albert' Faccini. In the Thirties when this photograph was taken by John Topham, Faccini had bout fifty barrel organ for hire at one shilling and sixpence a day, increasing to half-a-crown by the late Thirties.

ST. STEPHEN'S CHURCH

St. Stephen's Church, on the corner of Upper North Street, Poplar was a very high Church, being Anglo Catholic. The Vicar of St. Stephen's was the Reverend Mr. Pixell, and the Curate's name was Mr. Ponder. The Rev. Pixell's father often attended the services, but never took part in them, being so old, and short and tottery. Father Pixell was a thin man with drawn-in cheeks and very quiet, he seldom spoke unless he had to, but he was a very nice man, though stern.

Mr. Ponder was a jolly stout young man, though he had been in the 1914-1918 War and lost a leg. He had a false leg, and it was so well made that many people did not know he had a false leg, and even I didn't know until I was told by my mate. St. Stephen's was of Gothic style and was built of blocks of granite stone, some of which are now used as a wall at the corner of Upper North Street. It also had a fine hand pumped organ, which we choir boys had to take turns at, to pump either at the morning or evening service. There was also a fine big stained glass window behind the altar, and long narrow Gothic styled windows both sides of the church, all well coloured, especially the yellow, red and blue glass, which shone out brilliantly on a fine sunny day. Also on dark winter evenings, when the evening service was on, it was delightful to look at them from the outside.

The church hall was attached to the church by a Gothic styled covered arch, built of granite stone like the church. The church entrance was from East India Dock Road, being on the south side, and Upper North Street was at the altar end or east end. It only had a small entrance porch, entered by two steps and one into the church. The floor of the church was of black and red tiles, and on each side of the church were patterned iron gratings to let heat out in winter. There were two pulpits on each side of the choir stalls, of wood, having a round wooden stairway to each. And a fine accoustic sound board helped the congregation to hear some fine loud sermons.

The church had one big bell which was rung by two people, mostly choir boys, and I helped to ring it many a time.

I come to go to St. Stephen's Church through my school chum, Will Mew who lived in Pekin Street, Poplar. Besides being a choir boy, he worked for a doctor, taking bottles of medicine to the doctor's patients, and bringing back the empty bottles, and washing them. The square wicker basket he used was heavy, even without

70

the full bottles of medicine. Winter and summer he done it, in all weathers. Butcher's boys also carried baskets on their arms.

Many times I've walked through Rotherhithe Tunnel, and on to Blackwall Tunnel on the south side of the river with my mate Will Mew. Sometimes we played in the park over that side of the river, I think it was Southwark Park. This was during the summer holidays, I have walked the same route on my own as well.

BICYCLES

A form of transport often used in those days was cycling. There were many bikes to be seen besides the grocer's box tricycle which was also used by other tradespeople, and the butcher boy's two wheel bike, with baskets front and back loaded with meat and sausages.

The insurance man, rent collectors, baker's boy all used bikes. Most men and boys in their teens went to work by bike, and it was a common thing to see women and girls using a bike for travel to work. It would be a strange sound for me to hear the tinkle of a bicycle bell today, for all cyclists rang their bells when going round corners or approaching a group of people, or if anyone stood in his or her way. Even my doctor sometimes visited his patients by bike, and it was a common sight to see the parson on his bike visiting his parishioners.

The cycling clubs would go for a spin of a weekend, and it was a fine sight to see them on the country roads from the racing clubs to the mixed touring clubs with male and female cyclists together. They managed to cover many miles in a day considering the state of the roads. The tandem was another common type of bicycle and it was a nice sight to see a boy with his girl friend on the back pedalling along merrily on a country road or lane. Of course there was the cycle shop and repairers, where you could get any new part for your bike, and your bike could easily be repaired, and cheaply by a skilled mechanic, who did your repair thoroughly and satisfactorily.

Your cycle mechanic also repaired your gramophone, especially the spring which got stretched or broke through overwinding. For the gramophone was well used when I was young, and as soon as a family could afford it, they had one. Of course most were bought weekly, which was a natural thing for those days among poor people, but how enjoyable they made a party, or if you had the company of several young people come to your house. Of course the round cylinder type did not sound very good, the band or artists sounding very faint and far away, but the flat disc type was a great improvement. The sound box as well improved reproduction, making the music and singers sound much better, as the sound came through the horn. So the cycle mechanic was also the gramophone mechanic, and his shop window was filled with gramophone parts as well as cycle parts.

RECORDS, RADIO AND HOSPITAL

There was a cycle repairer in Three Colt Street, in fact there were two, but one of them let bikes out for hire as well. Westbrook's the paper shop also sold gramophones and records. The last record I bought at Westbrook's was called 'Felix Kept On Walking', it was on an Imperial record and cost 2/-, but I bought many of His Master's Voice records at 2/6d, which had good dance bands and orchestras on them, Jack Hylton, The Savoy Orpheans and later on, Ambrose were some of them.

RECORD LABELS FROM THE EARLY 1920s
Two versions of 'Limehouse Blues' by Jack Hylton's 'Queen's Dance Orchestra' recorded on the 16th of August and the 20th of September respectively. The difference in label credit is because Zonophone records sold at 2/- less than those marketed by the same company on the more prestigious HMV label.

J.E.Connor Collection.

The coming or invention of the radio was an eventful time. To be a radio amateur fan was all the rage after the 1914-1918 War, and round about 1922, nearly every one dashed home from work to put his or her earphones on, and by 1925-1926, everyone was listening to the B.B.C. jazz bands or orchestras. Around 1922-1923, men were keen on making their own crystal sets, and I had a crystal set made up for me by an amateur wireless fan, which consisted of a length of wire wound round a cardboard cylinder, which was attached to a piece of crystal. From that a wire went to the earphones. How I got a reception I don't know, of course the set was attached to an aerial, and nearly every back yard or garden had two poles with a long wire attached to them. Then when the valve sets came along, you often saw a person, man or woman, with an accumulator, which they had been to have recharged. But I will say it was the finest invention for lonely people, the blind and those in hospital.

About 1925, when I was getting on for 17 years of age, I was taken to St. George's Hospital, Wapping with Rheumatic Fever. I was kept on my back for ten weeks, not being allowed to sit up even, only having liquid food, first by a feeder, a thing like a small teapot, then after I was allowed to sit up, then get up, I had proper solid food. I was in the Hospital for three months, having only blanket baths, until the week I come out. The Doctor I was under was Doctor Carver, a young man. The Matron was a tall upright woman. November 11th happened when I was in there, and it was the Matron's inspection day, and when she came round she was wearing some medals and a row of ribbons.

The Sisters were very strict with the patients and very strict with the nurses, even the staff nurses. But they were taught and trained well. I know this from the sister doing some of her teaching to the nurses in the ward. I was kept on my back for ten weeks owing to a weak heart. The medicine I was given was soda-sal and cod liver oil and malt. The hospital was an old building having a coal fire in each ward. There were a lot of nurses employed there mostly Irish girls.

THREE COLT STREET
AND EMMETT STREET

How leisurely everything seemed in my childhood days, also there was class distinction so outstanding that it still stands out in my mind, both in wealth and positions. I suppose it was because I lived in a poor and working class area. There were many big families in those days, and if someone had a good job, there would be plenty of money coming in. The father would go out to work and the wife might have a small charring job, or work in a factory or minding children.

Then when the children grew up and went out to work, so the big money started to come in, and that is where some families like that started to look down at people, or think they were better than some. Of course, since there were no private cars and travel was mostly by tram or bus, the business people lived on their premises or near by. Men like foremen and managers lived closer to the poorer class, though they never mixed. Of course there were a lot of businesses in Limehouse, that's besides the big and small factories. There were all kinds of trade and manufacture done in Limehouse, and there were some interesting ones too, also in the neighbouring parishes of Ratcliff, Stepney, Poplar and Wapping.

One of the little businesses in Limehouse was at the top of Three Colt Street next to Dicker's the big jewellers and pawnshop, it was a sweet and grocery shop before it was knocked down, but when I was a boy I remember it as an ostrich feather cleaners and curlers, owned by a little old man and woman. In the shop window were two big glass domed cases. One held a big black ostrich feather, nicely curled and the other case held a white one. They also ironed stiff collars and cuffs of men's shirts. Some lady teachers and office workers used to wear stiff linen cuffs like men's stiff collars. These the little old couple cleaned and ironed as well.

I remember Mr. Marks the Justice of Peace for Limehouse. He had a baker's shop in Three Colt Street. He was a tall upright man, very smart in appearance and movement. Mrs. Marks was also tall and very ladylike, always wearing a high lace collar and a long black dress. The two daughters were tall and attended the Brunswick Chapel. A lot of women young and old went to the mothers' meetings at Brunswick Chapel, and they had a lot of outings from there in the summer.

There was a chemist in Three Colt Street, near the oil shop, whose name was Watts or Watkins. A clever chemist, who would make you up a prescription whatever your ailment, but he would tell you to go to the doctor, if you were too bad. Well he had two girls who wore blue mortar board school hats when going to school, and went to Howrah House Convent Girls School in East India Dock Road, where nuns and sisters done the teaching.

In Three Colt Street was a printers, named Peterken, and I remember being sent there to buy 2d or 1d worth of envelopes and writing paper. I think they printed the 'East End News' and placards advertising the football teams and rowing clubs, especially Millwall Reserves, which then played in Millwall. I saw them play many times when they were playing at home.

Pages, the tool and ironmongers, was a very big shop, which was on the corner of Ropemakers' Fields and Three Colt Street. In

Three Colt Street, next to Pages, was Beccles, the bacon and grocery shop, run by Mrs. Beccles, a widow and her son. Next to them was an Italian ice cream shop, and then a big empty space which was on the corner of Narrow Street. On the opposite corner of Narrow Street, being also the corner of Three Colt Street, was a big pub, where every morning except Sunday, a crowd of up to fifty men would be hanging around waiting to be called on to do a day's work on the Dundee and Aberdeen Wharves in Emmett Street, and the Dunbar Wharf in Narrow Street. As soon as the 'checker' or 'calling on' man came up, so there would be a big rush by the men, with their hands waving in the air, shouting out, "What about me!" or I'm here Bill!" or "Give us a chance!" until they were pointed at by the 'caller on' man. They would then go to the different wharves that the 'caller on' man was employed by, for their day or half day's work. This would be loading or unloading barges or ships, or trucking.

The paper shop in Emmett Street was opposite the entrance to Limehouse Pier. In their shop window they had the 'Police Gazette' and on the front it always showed an artist's picture of a gruesome murder in action, which had been committed. Inside were sporting articles with pictures of sportmen, boxers, jockeys etc. in action. Another paper shop, Harts in Three Colt Street, sold a lot of periodicals such as 'Titbits', 'Pearson's Weekly' and women's books with a paper pattern inside such as 'Weldons', 'Women's Weekly', 'Yes or No'. As well as books on hobbies and mechanics they sold trade books, such as the 'Barge Builder' and the 'Boilermaker'. At the top of Narrow Street, on the left hand side before turning left into Three Colt Street, was Sterry's the makers of mineral waters firm. As you went by you saw the machines filling the bottles of mineral water, some had a marble inside the bottle. It was not a very big firm and the owners lived above it.

Nearly all coffee shops and pubs gave away a time and tide table book, if they were near to the Thames, to their regular customers. These were handy little books for those working on the river, even a postman once told me that he had to know what time the tide would be on his round. The last one I had given to me was by the man and woman who owned the Dagger House coffee shop in Three Colt Street.

At one time this coffee shop was on the corner of Three Colt Street and the beginning of the Chinese Causeway, being opposite Potters Buildings. It must have been a converted pub at one time, as the name Dagger House was carved out in stone over the shop, and over the entrance to the shop was a big keystone and in the centre of the stone was carved a big dagger.

THE CHINESE CAUSEWAY

Chinese Causeway had a lot of Chinese living in the street, which was made up of shops on either side of the street. When these shops were closed the Chinamen moved in. One of the only shops still open was the English fishmonger, who had his own smoke hole, and smoked his own fish, such as herrings, haddocks and kippers. At the side of the shop was a narrow courtway leading to his smokehole and a few cottages. Opposite was a little Italian shop which sold fruit and icecream. Like in Pennyfields, the Chinamen were always gambling, so a lot of their places were turned into gambling dens. The roadway of the Causeway was of big cobbled stones, unevenly laid, and very awkward to walk on. The Causeway began from Three Colt Street, and when it reached Gill Street, it was very narrow, so that when a horse and cart went through, the wheels on either side touched the kerbs. Also one pavement was so narrow that only one person at a time could walk on it. This was the side where there were some houses. In Victorian times so my parents told me, this thoroughfare was a busy shoping centre, and market place. Starting from Three Colt Street, it continued as far as West India Dock Road.

Some of the young Chinese men were quite smart and well dressed in western clothes around the 1920's and 1930's. They had their straw hats complete with cord fixed to their jackets to stop the wind blowing them away, well fitted tailor made suits, smart collars, ties and well polished shoes.

One of their entertainments and pastimes would be for about a dozen young Chinamen to form a circle, and with a shuttle cock, pass it to one another with the back of their feet or a 'back kick'. I think the idea was to keep the shuttle cock in the air as long as they could. It was quite interesting and entertaining watching them.

Of course other Chinese were not so well dressed, and if you saw a lot of them just come off a ship, they seemed to be dressed very poor and shabby in their thin Chinese suits.

A noted gambling game in the Chinese Causeway and Pennyfields was 'Puck-a-Poo', you never saw the gamblers playing, but then when you wanted to have a gamble, you went to the place where it was going on, gave your betting money to a Chinese behind a counter, which was 6d in old money a bet, and you could have as many bets as you wanted. On paying your money, the Chinaman gave you a square sheet of paper, which was about 5 inches square, like a crossword, only with numbers where the black squares were.

Some numbers were green, others pale red, also some of these numbers were marked. So if your marked numbers corresponded with the 'bank's' sheet of numbers, you won. I don't know how much you won, not being keen on gambling. This explanation of the game was given to me by men and women who I knew and gambled on 'Puck-a-Poo' at the time in the 1920's. When the game was over then the 'bank was up', so you would see plenty of white men hanging around the Causeway, but more in Pennyfields, waiting for a 'bank' to come up. The pavement and road used to be well littered with 'Puck-a-Poo' papers at the time.

Now and then you heard of a police raid on the shut-up shops which were the gambling dens. You never saw any Chinese women, though you saw plenty of half-caste children, whose mothers lived with the Chinese. The Chinese were very fond of children, and it was a common sight to see them playing with the children. I saw a lot of the Chinese Causeway and Pennyfields, having to go through them to see my eldest sister, who was married and lived in a block of flats in Cotton Street Poplar.

West India Dock Road was a busy road. Besides the large amount of traffic going to and from the West India Docks, such as horse driven carts loaded with goods and merchandise going to and from the docks, there were foreign sailors of every nationality on the pavements. The fine big blond haired Danish and Swedish, also the Norwegian and Russian. I saw African and American coloured sailors, besides the white American and Dutch. There were also the Lascars in their bright coloured turbans, white tunics and gay sandals which turned up at the toes, not forgetting the Chinaman with his pigtail of jet black hair hanging down his back, and his hands tucked up his jacket sleeves. Some would go along with baskets or bags strung on a bamboo pole carried on their shoulders, sometimes a Chinaman would be at each end of the bamboo pole if it were heavily laden. Germans and Poles were also among those I saw.

CHURCH ROW

Church Row, or Newell Street now, only had a narrow roadway from Northey Street to The Mitre owing to houses on the left side having gardens in front of them, with very nice flowers growing in them. Some had big trees in them as well. On the corner of Northey Street and Church Row, was a big house with stables owned by Mr and Miss Banks, who lived there, and they had servants as well, besides a stable man. They owned a lot of property in Limehouse, Stepney, Ratcliff, Shadwell, Wapping and other districts. They rode about in a pony and trap to collect their rents, having a man to drive for them and look after the horse and trap while they collected the rents. They employed men to repair their property which they kept in good condition, having a big shed and yards in Oak Lane, which their property backed onto. After the 1914-1918 War, everything got dear, so that only one man and Mr. Banks repaired the property, until only Miss Banks was left to collect the rents on foot. This she did until she was attacked by some thugs, who stole her bag of rent money. This occurred after the last War, and she was very old then.

CHURCH ROW FROM THE RAILWAY BRIDGE   *(LONDON BOROUGH OF TOWER HAMLETS)*

Joseph King & Co., the boat builders, moved here in about 1912 from Three Colt Street when their old boat yard near Limekiln Dock was taken over by the L.C.C. to extend Gill Street School.

The full length of Church Row was from Commercial Road to Ropemakers' Fields, the latter end was very narrow, and on one corner was an old house, whose top part projected over the ground floor. the front part of the upper floors were all wooden, consisting of boards overlapping one another. Big wooden beams projected above the ground floor to support the upper floors and under the end of the wooden beams were stone supports, which were carved out into the shape of a cherub's face. The next house was built the same. Gas was the main street lighting, and a man with a pole which had a paraffin light on the top went around to light each lamp. Then in the morning he went round again to put them out. During the day he helped to clean the big glass lamps. Gas mantles were used, the same as those used in houses, except some houses which had inverted gas mantles.

The narrow entrance to Church Row had a ball topped post in the middle, though only two people side by side could get through, or a small donkey barrow, touching both brick walls. The first house on the right hand side was one you had to step down into from the street. Most very old houses had wooden partitions between the rooms inside, especially between the passage and the staircase.

CHURCH ROW
(LONDON BOROUGH OF TOWER HAMLETS)
Looking south towards the narrow entrance from Ropemakers' Fields - now part of the Barley Mow Estate. Church Lane first appears on Gascoyne's map of 1703 and was so called because it led to a path across the fields to the Parish Church of St. Dunstan's - Limehouse Church was not consecrated until 1730 - it became Church Row in 1875 and was renamed Newell Street in 1938, after J.E.Newell, a Stepney Borough Councillor from 1903 to 1930.

CHURCH ROW   (THE DICKENS HOUSE MUSEUM)

The Commercial Road end in about 1910. The second house from the right, with the continuous balcony, was the home of Charles Dickens' Godfather - Christopher Huffam, a prosperous sail maker and ship rigger. From about 1823, young Charles was a fairly regular visitor, being taken round Limehouse and on the River which fascinated him for the rest of his life and featured in several of the great novels. The site is now occupied by Limehouse Rectory, 5 Newell Street.

COURTS

Next to the first house in Church Row was a narrow court, only one person being able to enter, this court led into Three Colt Street, and a room of a house within the court was over each entrance to the court, although it widened out in the middle, three houses being on the left, a black wooden fence on the right with a door which had a lever latch to open it, but this door was nearly always open. It led into a courtyard paved with cobble stones and flag stones, with a water stand-pipe in the middle. There may have been about six small houses round the yard, but I'm not sure, but I have seen women and children get water from the stand-pipe.

Nearly opposite the court on the other side of Three Colt Street was another court called Gun Square, with a one person entrance. Simmon's grocery and coal merchant shop had a bedroom over the court entrance. The court was narrow at the entrance by the shop, but widened out into a square, no more than eight feet wide. The houses were built the same as Willow Row. At the other end was another courtway leading from Gun Lane or Grenade Street, as it is now called. It had an arched shape entrance just wide enough for a small pony and cart to get through. The house on the left, and the grocers shop on the right had two steep stone steps, as they both had underground cellars. Also the shop's bedroom was over the archway.

Next to the grocers shop was a small barbers shop, no steps, where I got my hair cut when I was a boy for 1½d old money, close crop front fringe. Small boys had a wooden monkey up a stick or a tumbling clown or a whistle given to them by the barber, who also sold comics, 'Chips' and 'Funny Wonder' etc. There were also a lot of Italian barbers as well, but they charged 2d and had no toys.

The entrance to the archway had two granite corner stones, and big uneven cobble stones to walk on, the corner stones or gate stones were always each side of a firm's back yard gates where the traffic entered or left. The reason being that they stopped the cart wheels from scraping against the brickwork of the gates. These stones were always of hard granite stone, being about one an a half foot high and a foot wide, and rounded off at the top. The stone yard in Northey Street used to make these stones.

TAYLOR WALKER'S

The big brewery Taylor Walker's had a lot of horses and brewer's drays, and I well remember the loaded carts full of hops that had been used, being taken away steaming hot. Where they took them or what they used them for I don't know, but they must have been of some use. Also there used to be white clouds of foam rising up from where they were brewing sometimes, and there was always the strong smell of hops. The used hops always came out from the Northey Street gates and the big sacks of fresh hops went in the same gates.

There was also a big weighbridge and weighbridge office at these gates and also the brewery offices. The stables were in Ropemakers' Fields, on the other side facing the brewery. There was a carpentry shop in one of the buildings on this side. Near where the brewing was done were big loading bays with stages as high as the drays, so that the big and small barrels of beer, ales and porter could be rolled straight on to the drays. Both horse and dray were under cover, also on the stages were spiral chutes to send the crates of bottled beer or ales from the floors above. It used to be ever so busy and noisy as you went by when loading and unloading was going on.

Before you got to the loading bays there were two wide gates, always open, on the left of these gates was the cooperage, and we could see and hear the men banging away at the wooden barrels. In the big yard we could see men rolling barrels about, many men worked there and were employed by Taylor Walker's.

TAYLOR WALKER BEER LABEL

An example from the Barley Mow Brewery which shows the Art Deco influence that was fashionable between the wars.

J.E.Connor Collection

82

OAK LANE

Oak Lane began as far back as Globe Alley and was separated from Northey Street by the stone yard, where they made the cobble stones to shape and size for the roads. Also, the kerb stones and paving stones were made here, so some people called it 'the paving yard'. When the gates were open, you saw the stone masons at work, chipping away at the kerb stones, and cobble stones, and also cutting the paving stones to shape and size. Some of the men wore goggles, some didn't wear any. They worked in their shirt sleeves rolled up, an old sack tied round their waist, these generally reaching down to their hob nailed boots. From a back view of the men, you saw the leather strap just below the knee of their mole skin trousers. Some wore corduroy trousers, wearing the strap just the same. In Winter, the men wore an old jacket or overcoat to keep warm, for they worked in the open all the time, except when it rained, then they worked under a large shed, which was open at one end. The cobbles were stacked neatly when they were finished, but the chipping and cutting of the stones and kerbs was done on a large round stone, nearly two feet thick, and the height of a man's waist. Others were chipped and cut on a square shaped table. Some men sat among the unfinished cobbles or kerbs and chipped away as they sat on an old sack. The yard had no wall, but galvanized iron sheets and any old tin as a partition.

It was interesting watching the men chipping away at the different stones, stopping now and then to eye their work. They had no ruler, or at any rate I don't remember them having any, but they used a finished stone as a sample, and there was constant tapping and chipping all the time.

The stone yard was shifted to Medland Street, next to an alley way which led into Narrow Street. Opposite the Medland Street end, was the White Hart pub. The stone yard, alley and other buildings reaching to Medland Hall, is where the Stepney Borough Garage was built.

The first factory in Oak Lane on the Limehouse Cut side was a scrap firm. This was originally a German firm. They collected the scrap tin from the tin box factories, the tin toy firms, tin can firms and others. The scrap tin was put into presses and formed into square bales, which were sent to the metal firms to be melted down. I think a lot of this scrap tin went into Germany, for the firm closed down during the 1914-1918 War. The other firm that did this kind of work was the London Electron Works, which was the first firm in Horseferry Road, which you turned into from Narrow Street. This firm was British, and did not move 'till a long while after the War, then they went Barking way, and are still manufacturing. The firm next to the tin firm in Oak Lane was Fullers the timber merchants. They had a big fire during the 1914-1918 War, which caused them to close down. These firms backed onto the Cut, so that some of their merchandise was brought up by barge or taken away by barge.

On the other side of the Cut was the Island Lead Mills. Well, a gun used to go off from there exactly at 10.00 o'clock. The reason that the gun was fired at that time of night, was because the firm had lost a lot of lead at different times through robberies, so the owner made a threat that he would shoot anyone trying to steal lead from the firm. Well, by chance, his son went out one evening without letting his parents know. When he came back he tried to get indoors without being seen. By chance, his father was standing at the street door, so seeing the figure creeping about in the dark, he ran indoors, got his gun and fired at the figure, who happened to be his son. It happened at exactly 10.00 pm, so as a memorial of the tragedy, they had a gun go off exactly at that time.

Next to the timber yard were a couple of houses, the front of these houses faced the Cut, so the occupants of them had to go in the back way. You turned left then, still in Oak Lane, which was at the back of Northey Street School, but if you continued on, there was a cul-de-sac, where there was a blacksmith's and two houses. Many a time, I have watched the smithy hammering away on the anvil, pumping the bellows of the fire up, and shoeing the horses. For this smithy used to shoe and put new tips on the Cut horses, that pulled the barges up and down the Cut. Instead of going down the cul-de-sac you turned right and went through an alley into Northey Street. In this alley were two or three houses which backed on to the school. In one of these houses there lived a blind man, who earned his keep by begging. He had a brass plate hung on him, with the word 'Blind' on it. this was to certify that he was a licenced beggar. He had been employed as a brewer's drayman, and while sitting on the back of the brewer's dray, the carman drew his whip back to make a lash at the horses, to make them go faster, and in doing so, the whip caught Mr. Moss, (that was the drayman's name) across the eyes, blinding him instantly. the brewery firm bought the licence for him to beg for life. He had a son named Tom, and he was one of the boys I played with after school. For he went to the Church School in Dixon Street, and I was at Northey Street.

On the other side of Northey Street was Brightlingsea Place

where I lived. It started as a wide alley. On the corner was the Experienced Fowler, a big public house, which was owned by Taylor Walker's, the big brewery near the beginning of Northey Street. The Experienced Fowler was a big pub, and it did a very good trade, especially in beer and ales. The licencee's name was Selby, he had been a shipwright. It was taken over by his son Jim.

THE EXPERIENCED FOWLER   *(LONDON BOROUGH OF TOWER HAMLETS)*

Taken on 13th January 1930, the photograph shows Jim Selby's daughter in the doorway, prior to demolition for an extension of the Stepney Borough Council's Electricity Station. One of many Taylor Walker's pubs in the neighbourhood, its front was probably rebuilt about 1876 when Northey Street was extended westwards by the Limehouse District Board of Works.

WILLOW ROW

The three houses in Willow Row before the stables had no back yards. They had two rooms, one down and one up, and a small room with a water tap and a small sink and toilet. The Butlers lived in the first house, they had two sons killed in the 1914-1918 War, the Murphys next who had four children, then the Coles with two children. The stables had enough room inside for a small cart and at the back were three pony stalls, not big enough to hold a big cart horse, so I only saw a pony or donkeys stabled there. Henry Forrow, who had a fruit and green grocers shop in Brightlingsea Place was the only person I knew who kept a pony and cart in the stables, and also sometimes he had donkeys and donkey barrows kept there, although sometimes the barrows were outside his shop. He married a girl who lived in the upstairs of the wooden sided house in Chivers Court, called Clark. Downstairs were the Nugents. Mary Nugent married Bill Higgins, whose mother owned the Grapes public house in Narrow Street. He worked for his mother behind the bar, then taking over from her when she retired.

WILLOW ROW IN THE THIRTIES   *(TOPHAM)*

John Topham's photograph shows numbers 6 to 9, the four one up and one down houses past Henry Forrow's stables on the right; with Ben's Infant School beyond and the single story cottages at the end and the back yard wall of the Northey Street houses on the right. The lantern roof of the Barley Mow Brewery is seen in the top right of the picture. 'Buzz' Rogers who worked at the Paperboard Mills lived in the first house, where his wife is sitting outside chatting to Mrs. Mackey from next door. The man in the street is 'Whitey' who kept a stall in Salmon Lane and went round the streets selling winkles and shrimps. This end of Willow Row and the neighbouring courts was known locally as the Orchard and was demolished in 1938.

Of the four houses in Willow Row past the stables, you walked into the living room from the street door, facing the street door was the door to the tiny kitchen,having a gas stove in the far wall in front of the little old fireplace. Some had a gas stove between the small sink and the yard door. All the tenants got their water from a tap outside in the little yard, a window was over the sink.

In the living room was a fireplace with oven and next to it in a corner was a tiny staircase which led to a front bedroom over the living room. At the back was a small bedroom over the kitchen. The brick copper was in the yard under a small wooden shelter for when it rained.

Next to the stables was Granny Rogers and husband, the Mackeys, next the Cakebreads, a widower with two sons, then the Stanleys, a big family. Turning right facing the school, the first family's name was Lyal, who had two sons and one girl, then the Carlaws, a big family, Simmons next, and the Moets in the last house, then you went into Chivers Court.

CHIVERS COURT

In Chivers Court were Berlins the builders, they had no gas lamp, only paraffin and his two barrows would be outside the house. Next lived a lady with two girls but no gas, both families had pianos. Next were the Clarks, they had gaslight and four sons, these houses were built the same as the eight houses in Willow Row, but had very long gardens from which you could get into Ropemakers' Fields.

Opposite the Square in Chivers Court was a space left by demolished houses and on it, on Sunday mornings or sometimes all day, men used to gamble, several groups of them, women as well among them. Next to these 'ruins' were three tall old houses on three floors, the end one having a wooden side. There lived a lady with two girls named Forrow, whose husband was killed in the 1914-1918 War, who was the sister-in-law of Henry Forrow the greengrocer of Brightlingsea Place. These three tall houses in Chivers Court helped to form the Square, and facing them were two little houses like those in Willow Row past the stables. They had a small yard from which you could get into Brightlingsea Place, which the tenants used. Mrs. Britain had the first her son was killed in the 1914-1918 War, then there were the Sambrooks, a big family of girls and boys, next to Sanders carpentry shop and stables. This Square was well used by boys to play football, it had a couple of smooth long granite stones, so in winter when the square was snowed over we used to have slides on the long stones.

In the middle of the three tall houses in Chivers Court lived Mr. Joblin, a tall elderly man who done odd jobs for a living, but worked at ship repairing when he was young, like his son who lived nearly opposite him in the Square. Mr. Joblin did odd jobs like boot and shoe repairs, watch and clock repairs and locks, in fact he was a clever handy man. His daughter and granddaugher lived in the middle floor in two rooms, her husband was killed in the 1914-1918 War. In the house next door lived the Finns, having three girls and two boys. On their middle floor of two rooms were a married couple, Mr. and Mrs. Skinner, with two children a boy and a girl, the husband was a steam train engine driver, his wife's parents owned the oil shop in Three Colt Street, opposite Grenade Street.

Off Chivers Court was a small court which had a wooden door entrance. On the right side when entering were five cottages which had a front yard. These cottages backed onto the cottages in Willow Row facing the Infants School. They were built the same as Willow Row. Three of the families which lived in them were the Wigmore's and the Martin's, and a big family the Norris's.

There were four houses in the Square which backed onto the little court. In the first were the Barretts, mother, father, three girls and one boy. The father was a 'poker' in the Regent's Dock. This job was to put a barge beside a ship to be loaded with goods from the ship, or goods from a barge onto a ship, or from a warehouse onto a barge. Some goods were brought to the Dock by a string of barges, others were taken out into the Thames. Some barges were taken through the Regent's Canal loaded with goods from the ships in the Regent's Dock.

Next to the Barretts in Chivers Court Square were the Clarks, with grown up sons and daughters. Upstairs lived Mrs. Darby, a widow and her daughter. Next to old Joblin's son and wife, who had three sons and a daugher, was a lady whose name I never knew, but upstairs lived Mrs. Marshall who had three sons and two daughters all grown up. There was a name cut out on these houses, it said 'Triggs Place 1823'.

The Willmotts lived in Chivers Court Square before the Joblins, they were a big family of girls and boys. They moved to Batson Street, where Limehouse railway station was. Next to the station was a tall shed and yard where they hung sailing ship sails, which were made by women who were employed by a firm of sailmakers, which was under the railway arch in the turning called The Mitre

'CHIVERS COURT SQUARE'   *(THE DICKENS HOUSE MUSEUM)*

Mr. Barrett the 'poker' lived in the first house on the right of the terrace which formed the east side of the Square, until the Electricity Station was extended and Brightlingsea Place was relaid through the Square, as seen in this photograph of about 1934. On the far right is the corner of Faraday House built on the site of the Chivers Court 'ruins' for families from the old Brightlingsea Place. Part of Northey Street School is seen on the far left and in the middle of the terrace is the stone which bore the inscription 'Trigg's Place 1823' – this was the name of the Square up until 1894 when it became part of Chivers Court.

REGENTS CANAL DOCK IN THE THIRTIES   *(THE WATERWAYS MUSEUM)*

The ship is moored alongside the East Quay, discharging her cargo into a lighter with others being 'poked' into position. The road under the London & Blackwall Railway bridge is Mill Place, leading to Commercial Road. This northern half of the Dock is to be infilled for luxury flats – a sad end for London's main entrance to the English canals.

BRIGHTLINGSEA BUILDINGS AND THE POWER STATION

Brightlingsea Buildings in Brightlingsea Place was built in about 1906 and some very respectable people lived there when I was young. I well remember the District Nurse living in them, office workers and men wearing collar and tie, bowler or trilby hat going to work, who must have been craftsmen of some sort or another. Most boys who lived in the Buildings had peaked pimple hats, no caps and blue serge suits, and most also had Norfolk suits. Boys and girls from the Buildings attended Northey Street School and were very bright at their lessons, so on prize giving day they generally received a book or medal. Some won scholarships and went either to Thomas Street School or George Green's School, where the teaching was of a higher standard, including foreign languages.

It was in Brightlingsea Buildings that Major Attlee had a flat on the ground floor, I suppose using the flat as his headquarters. It was just after the 1914-1918 War. Major Attlee still wore his officer's uniform. He was a smart man, not very tall, as he was shorter than the men with him. Two other officers were with him sometimes, besides the men in civilian clothes. It was at the time of a General Election and the voting or polling station was at Northey Street School. Major Attlee was the Labour candidate for Limehouse, he won. Mr. Marks the baker was the Liberal candidate, I don't remember the Conservative candidate.

1922 GENERAL ELECTION LETTER
(LONDON BOROUGH OF TOWER HAMLETS)

Attlee promised to tell Parliament that the people of Limehouse were sick and tired of toiling long hours for low pay and being condemned to live in poverty and squalor. He was duly elected and served as the MP for Limehouse for twenty eight years.

THE MAN FOR LIMEHOUSE

C.R. ATTLEE.
The Labour Candidate.

The Stepney Electricity Station as it was called when it was built was a noisy dirty building, having a loud dynamo which caused a lot of vibration and a lot of noise from the machinery. The big pile of coal to feed the fires was kept in the open at the Northey Street end. The coal was in very small pieces, and when it was windy, the coal dust used to blow about and get in your eyes. In the street, people had to walk on the coal grit, we even got it in the houses. Also the vibration of the machinery was so great, that it vibrated our coal fire oven door so much we had to have a piece of newspaper between the oven and the oven door to stop it rattling. Even an empty cup in a saucer rattled.

The station or 'electron' as some people called it, backed on to Globe Alley. Among the families who lived in Globe Alley were the Keilys and the Curtises, also the Lows. On the Brightlingsea Place side, there were corrugated sheets of iron along the side of the power station, and during the 1914-1918 War it was a common thing to hear shrapnel banging against it.

STEPNEY ELECTRICITY STATION FROM REGENT'S CANAL DOCK

(THE WATERWAYS MUSEUM)

A string of narrow boats waiting to load in 1933. The Island Lead Mills are on the left and in the background, the Electricity Station built by the Stepney Borough Council in 1909. Globe Alley was on the right of this building but disappeared during the extension to Shoulder of Mutton Alley. A 350 foot chimney was built in 1937, in response to complaints about the smoke and dirt from the low chimneys seen in the photograph.

In the 1920's there was still gas street lighting, even in the streets and alleys around the power station. There were two extensions to the power station and I well remember the first one in the 1920's when new and extra machinery was put in. Big low trollys brought the machinery, these were owned by the railway companies or heavy cartage contractors, and were pulled by two, three or even four horses. There were big transformers, dynamos and other kinds of machinery. Some big metal parts for boilers. Big cylinder parts for big piping were kept where the old stone yard was, and many a time I've enjoyed myself with other boys climbing about the big iron parts. The next big extention was in the 1930's when they pulled the houses down in Brightlingsea Place and put us people in a block of flats called Faraday Dwellings.

SHOULDER OF MUTTON ALLEY

The next turning to Globe Alley was Shoulder of Mutton Alley. In this turning there was the flock mills, where they made up the flock mostly for the flock beds and upholstery. Big bales of old woollen rags mostly, but also linen and cotton rags would be brought there. These rags were sorted, metal buttons and buckles were cut off them. The first operation after undoing the bales and taking out any bits of wood or metal that had got mixed up in the rags was to put the rags into a big boiler, where they were washed and boiled thoroughly, I don't know how long, but one employee told me nearly all day or night. The cleaned rags were put in a big cylinder which had big cutting knives and went round and round cutting the rags into pieces.

From that machine the rags were put into a machine called a kneader, which kneaded them into flock. When the drying process was done, I'm not sure if it was straight after the rags were washed and boiled or when they were flock. The machines must have been driven by steam, and when the stoker brought out his ashes, he would hose them down with water as the ashes would be put in front of the mill where horses and carts went by. They could not be put at the back of the mill, as it backed onto the houses in Globe Alley, so when the ashes were brought out and hosed, boys including myself, used to search among them for very good brass, steel and tin buttons to play with. There were different kinds of flock and grades, the best was white flock. There were a lot of uses for it besides for filling beds and pillows. Wyatts, the furniture and bedding shop in Salmon Lane, on the corner of Rhodeswell Road, had four chairs outside their shop window, with samples of different kinds of flock on them in big brown paper bags for you to choose from. At the far end of Pennyfields was a ships bedding firm called Wilsons who bought most of their flock from the Shoulder of Mutton flock mills. The sailors nickname for a mattress was a 'donkey'. The flock mills moved to Branch Road between the Mortuary and the Finnish Sailors' Mission, when Stepney Power Station was extended.

At the top of Shoulder of Mutton Alley, that's the Narrow Street end was Pintsch's the brass founders, a German firm that turned out some highly skilled work. The other part of the firm was on the other side of Narrow Street, the side of Kidney Stairs, an opening to the river. In Narrow Street between Shoulder of Mutton Alley and Globe Alley were two houses. These projected out causing the road to be narrow, and only wide enough for a horse and cart to go through, the same as at the beginning of Ropemakers' Fields.

THE PAPERBOARD MILLS

I had been working for about two years at the Limehouse Paperboard Mills, when one of the owners, Mr. Sidney Hough, got killed when he was horse riding. He included his employees in his will, so one pay day, I received my pay packet, also an envelope with my name typewritten on it, and inside was a paper saying, 'Mr. Sidney Hough has bequested to Benjamin Thomas, the sum of £2.10s.0d'. I kept the paper until our flat got bombed twice, when we lost a lot of valuables, furniture and books. I was in the army abroad when it happened.

Mr. Sidney Hough was a smart man, very active, with a fresh rosy cheeked face. He said a cheery, "Good morning" to us employees. He always wore a white silk cravat. His son Harold took over from him, another good employer.

The length of Hough's offices in Narrow Street had a tarry block road in front of it. This must have been for quietness against the noise of the horse and cart traffic. A little further up was Lockside. On one corner was a big pub. Hough's employed a lot of women at one time, who sorted out the waste paper, old bags and old rope, especially during the 1914-1918 War, and it was a common sight to see the pub packed with many women as well as men. Next to this pub I can't remember the name of it, I think it may have been the Bricklayers' Arms, was a little grocers who also sold sweets, besides being a cafe as well, in that they sold cheese 3d, ham 4d and corn beef 3d, sandwiches. You could also buy a 1d packet of Lyons tea, 1d of Milk, 1d of sugar to make a can of tea with. You could also buy 3d of tea in your own billy can.

From Waters the tea shop were houses which continued up to Northey Street. The other side of Narrow Street facing Lockside was a small pub called the Watermans Arms, and to enter the pub for a drink, the men had to duck their heads, as the door was so low, and go down two steps, so that they could stand upright inside. This pub was used by lightermen mostly and was at the mouth of the Limehouse Cut.

MILL WORKERS IN THE THIRTIES   (MR. BILL COLE)

Standing at the back are Steve Thompson, second from left; Flack, fourth from left; and Bill Humphries and Marney at the end of the row. Sitting on the kerb are Fred Collier, second from the left; with Chris Dagonite next and A. Osborne. Hough's workers were noted for their strength and long service.

VISITORS

Many notable people and royalty have come to or passed through Limehouse, and it was to my dismay that I was unable to see many of them. But I was lucky enough to see King George and Queen Mary, when they rode through the East End of London in celebration of their Silver Jubilee. Their majesties rode through Burdett Road from the Commercial Road to Mile End Road. I was on the Limehouse Cut Bridge. When they passed me I waved and shouted, "Hooray!" like all the rest of the people who lined the route. Some shouted, "Good old George! Good old Mary!", for they were greatly loved by everyone, and no-one showed it more than the East Ender.

SILVER JUBILEE DRIVE   (LONDON BOROUGH OF TOWER HAMLETS)

King George V and Queen Mary passing along Burdett Road in an open landau, with an escort of Life Guards on Saturday 25th May 1935; having just met the Mayors of Stepney, Bethnal Green, Hackney, Poplar and Shoreditch at Limehouse Town Hall.

I was in the Burdett Road, when the King's son George VI and Queen Elizabeth rode through to celebrate peace and the winning of the 1939–1945 World War. Queen Mary graciously bowed or nodded her head, and at other times gently waving her hand as she was driven by her coach pulled by a four horse team. The procession started with the police on horseback, then came the King and Queen Mary's body guard on horseback, and how brilliant they looked in their bright red coats, snow white bandoliers, shiny black boots and highly polished helmets. The Queen's lady in waiting was in the coach as well.

I heard Oswald Mosely give a couple of speeches at the blackshirt meetings at the top of Salmon Lane, outside the Sailors' Home just before the 1939-1945 War. A lot of people attended these meetings, but not many Limehouse people, except young teenagers and 'yobboes' who wanted a bit of excitement. Of course people from outside Limehouse were in the crowd, and at one big meeting at Salmon Lane, a lot of people came in cars, some cars were Rolls Royces and other limousines. A lot of police were there to control the crowd as well.

WEDDINGS

Many couples got married in Limehouse Church, being taken there by horse drawn cab, but most who lived near the Church walked there and back after the marriage service. It was a common sight to see wedding parties walking from the church after the service. Of course the bride didn't wear a lace train or veil, but a dress or costume. Some couples lived a good way away from the Church, and I have seen many wedding parties going back to the wedding breakfast by tram. I have seen three or four wedding parties going to and from the Church on the same tram that I have been riding on.

MARIE VINCENT'S WEDDING   (MRS. ANNE IRVING & MRS. BARBARA GOGGIN)

The wedding party outside the bride's family home at 7 Drewton Street, Ratcliffe, about 1920. The pub on the corner of Devonport Street is seen on the left with the London & Blackwall Railway arches on the right of the photograph.

Easter and Christmas were two of the most popular times of the year for weddings. Besides the church, the beershops and public houses were very busy, and the publicans made plenty of money for themselves. The little money lenders done well out of weddings sometimes. For some families tried to act big and have all their children in new clothes, and couples had a lot of children in them days. A lot of beer was got in for the celebrations, besides spirits. Whisky and gin was much cheaper then, in fact most people kept a drop of whisky or port wine in their houses.

In the evening the family, relations and friends of the wedding party used to go to a nearby pub. As the time went on, so the pub got livelier. There would be singing, dancing, loud laughter and people joking with one another. Then at closing time, the customers would come rolling out, some were as drunk as could be, some women got drunk as well as the men, and they would all start singing all the way home. I have seen many a row and fight going on at a wedding party.

My eldest sister Mag had a walking wedding in 1912, and my eldest brother Bill was married in his army uniform in 1914. My sister Nora was married in 1919, my brother Sid in 1920, and my sister Grace in 1921. These were all walking weddings, although my brother Sam and I had white weddings with cars. Sam in 1938 and me in 1942. When my sister Nora married the whole length of the altar rail was taken up with couples, the same with my brother Sid, but I have been told there has even been two rows at Limehouse Church.

The reason couples got married at holiday times was that they could then have the holiday Monday to get over it, for couples couldn't afford to go away for a honeymoon then. They could not afford a week off from work, and in the 1920's when people got a week's holiday, they could only afford to go to Southend, Brighton or Margate for their honeymoon. To think couples fly to Italy, France or Spain and other places for their honeymoon these days.

CAYLEY STREET

MATLOCK STREET

B. Guardians'
Offices

P.H. CHASELEY STREET

YORK

SQUARE

WAKELING STREET

School

FARNHAM STREET

FARNHAM STREET

LOWELL STREET

Salmon Lane

School

Brunton's
Wharf

Salmon's
Wharf

Commercial Road
Bridge

C.B.

Rose Lane

LONDON & BLACKWALL RAILWAY

North Quay

Stepney Junc.
Station

LONDON & BLACKWALL RAILWAY

Limehouse
Junc.

Lion Wharf

East Quay

ROSE LANE

Trav. Crane

WHITE HORSE ROAD

Regent's Canal
Dock

Dolphin

Jetty

South East Quay

Warehouse

Saw Mill

Jetty

REGENT'S CANAL
DOCK

Wharves

Public
Baths

Oyster Stores

Seamen's
Mission

Medland Quay

Trav. Crane

South Quay

Jetty

BUTCHER ROW

St. James's
Church

ST. JAMES'S
GARDENS

HORSEFERRY BRANCH ROAD

Trav.
Crane

HORSEFERRY ROAD

LONDON STREET

P.H. MEDLAND STREET

Locks

Biscuit
Works

Brewery

NARROW

Keeper's
Wharf

Ratcliff
Cross
Stairs

Wharves

Old Sun
Wharf

Chinnock's
Wharf

Regent's Canal
Entrance

Victoria Wharf

Dolphin

Limehouse Cut
Entrance

Ratcliff Cross
Wharf

Mud

Mud

Stairs

Reduced from the original Ordnance Survey 1:2500 map to a scale of
approximately 1:4340 (or about 15 inches to a mile).
This Edition published by Alan Godfrey, Dunston, Gateshead in 1986.

Met. Boro. Bdy.

LIMEHOUSE SOUTH WARD

LIMEHOUSE

CALCUTTA ST.
FARRANCE STREET
School
Baptist Chapel
Hippodrome
Langley House Home for Orphans
Bank

Copenhagen Place
Britannia Bridge
Limehouse Town Hall
Recreation Ground
St. Anne's Church
G.Ya. (Dis.)
Church Inst.
D.Fn.

Copenhagen Wharf
Col. Zinc
Rubber and Works
Bridge Wharf
Crane
St. Anne's Wharf
Sailors' Palace
Strangers' Home
Seamen's Laundry
Tel. Exc. G.P.O.
Police Station

B.M. 25·3
Bank
B.M. 20·1

THREE COLT STREET
CHURCH ROW
THE MITRE
Sun. Sch.
Chapel

GRENADE STREET
Hall
Trinidad Street
ROBERT STREET
SALTER STREET

Barley Mow Brewery
ROPEMAKERS FIELDS
School
PHOEBE STREET
Lange Street
Lion Works
St. Peter's Church

LIMEKILN DOCK
Dundee Wharf
Danby Wharf Wharves
Mud
W.M.

Albion Wharf
School
Sequoia Wharf
Norway Wharf
ROW

Duke Shore Steps
Duke Shore Wharf
Septic Tanks
Wharves
Anchor Wharf

Limehouse Pier
Limehouse Hole Stairs
River Front Wharf
Dolphin
Aberdeen Wharf
Custom
Crane
Cranes Wharf
ROWLEY STREET
EMMETT STREET
DOCK
Mud

RAGGED SCHOOL MUSEUM TRUST

The purpose of the Ragged School Museum Trust is to make the unique history of the East End of London, and in particular of the Copperfield Road Ragged School, accessible to all members of the general public.

The Ragged School Museum Trust was founded in 1983. The Ragged School Museum was opened in 1990 in three Victorian canal-side warehouses in Copperfield Road, East London. These buildings were previously used by Dr Barnardo to house the largest ragged school in London.

In a re-created classroom of the period visitors can now experience for themselves how Victorian children were taught. There are also displays on local history, industry and life in the East End and a varied programme of temporary exhibitions.

The museum runs a variety of different activities for all ages. These include workshops, history talks, treasure hunts and canal walks. These are open to all.

Opening Times
Wednesday & Thursday   10.00am - 5.00pm
1st Sunday of each month   2.00pm - 5.00pm
Admission is free but donations are appreciated.

For further information please contact:
Ragged School Museum, 46-50 Copperfield, London E3 4RR.
Tel: 0181-980 6405

L3G

Patrons: Dame Gillian Wagner DBE, Lord Briggs, Bruce Oldfield, Lord Murray

Registered Charity No. 800538 and a company Limited by Guarantee No. 2308621